Hodder Geogr...

Series Editor: JEFF BATTERSBY   Series Consultant: R...

WEATHER, CLIMATE & ECOSYSTEMS

David Elcome

Hodder & Stoughton

A MEMBER OF THE HODDER HEADLINE GROUP

Acknowledgements

The publishers would like to thank the following for giving permission to reproduce copyright photographs in this book: BBC, 1.1; Science Photo Library, 1.3, 1.4, 1.19, 1.20, 1.21, 1.25, 1.26, 2.1, 2.5, 2.7, 3.19, 4.11a,b,c,d; Corbis, 1.14, 2.9a,b, 4.2, 4.3, 4.7; Bruce Coleman, 1.17, 3.1, 3.8, 3.11, 3.13, 3.14, 3.15, 3.17, 3.18, 4.5, 4.6, 4.9; The Meteorological Office, 2.6, 2.8, 2.10; Hutchinson, 3.5, 3.16, 3.20; Action Plus, 4.10.

All other photos supplied by the author, David Elcombe.

Every effort has been made to contact the holders of copyright material used in this book, but if any have been overlooked, the publishers will be pleased to make the necessary alterations at the first opportunity.

Orders: please contact Bookpoint Ltd, 39 Milton Park, Abingdon, Oxon OX14 4TD. Telephone: (44) 01235 400414, Fax: (44) 01235 400454. Lines are open from 9.00 – 6.00, Monday to Saturday, with a 24 hour message answering service. Email address: orders@bookpoint.co.uk

British Library Cataloguing in Publication Data
A catalogue record for this title is available from The British Library

ISBN 0 340 701986

First published 1998
Impression number   10 9 8 7 6 5 4 3 2
Year   2004 2003 2002 2001 2000 1999

Copyright © 1998

All rights reserved. No part of this publication may be reproduced or transmitted in any form or by any means, electronic or mechanical, including photocopy, recording, or any information storage and retrieval system, without permission in writing from the publisher or under licence from the Copyright Licensing Agency Limited. Further details of such licences (for reprographic reproduction) may be obtained from the Copyright Licensing Agency Limited, of 90 Tottenham Court Road, London W1P 9HE.

Cover photo from Robert Harding

Typeset by Wearset, Boldon, Tyne & Wear
Printed in Hong Kong for Hodder & Stoughton Educational, a division of Hodder Headline Plc, 338 Euston Road, London NW1 3BH by Colorcraft Ltd.

CONTENTS

Chapter 1
Weather – what is it, and what causes it?   Pages 1–21

Chapter 2
Measuring the Weather   Pages 22–31

Chapter 3
Ecosystems   Pages 32–47

Chapter 4
The changing climate and environmental issues   Pages 48–58

Glossary   Pages 59–60

HODDER GEOGRAPHY – Weather, Climate & Ecosystems

WEATHER – WHAT IS IT, AND WHAT CAUSES IT?

Key Idea

The weather has a great influence on our everyday lives – it affects us in all sorts of ways all of the time. But what do we really know about it? What causes the weather? How do weather forecasters know what to expect? What is the difference between weather and climate? This chapter looks at the different forms that weather can take.

"Here is the Weather Forecast...

... for Wednesday, 17th December. Winter has us in its icy grip for the moment. Over Eastern Europe there is high pressure and in Moscow temperatures have fallen to −29° C! They won't be quite as low in Britain, thank goodness, but it will feel bitterly cold today. The 'wind-chill factor' will make it appear colder than it really is. For the southern half of England and Wales there is a severe weather warning. Snow can be expected during the morning and there may be blizzard conditions for a while. Later in the day, however, the snow will turn to sleet and rain as milder air spreads in from the south. Elsewhere in the country there will be isolated snow flurries, followed by a period of more persistent snow before milder weather arrives during the evening.

The outlook is for milder weather, with showers and longer spells of rain in most places during the next few days, as a 'Low' with several associated 'fronts' approaches Britain from over the Atlantic."

RESOURCE 1.1
Michael Fish giving the weather forecast

Forecasting the weather

The weather experienced by a place on any particular day depends on the Earth's atmosphere – its temperature, the pressure of the air and the amounts of water vapour in it (see **Resource 1.5**). The information is gathered by weather recording stations, aircraft, ships, oil rigs at sea and satellites that orbit the Earth. Other vital data comes from *radiosondes*, packages of electronic instruments carried by weather balloons up to heights of 30,000 metres, and *radar stations*, which keep track of the movements of storms and heavy rainfall. By monitoring the condition of the atmosphere and predicting how it is likely to change during the next few hours and days, weather forecasters are able to suggest what the weather is likely to be. Most forecasts are very accurate for the 12 hours ahead, but very local factors can upset their general predictions and there can be sudden, unexpected variations. It is very difficult to make accurate long-term forecasts.

RESOURCE 1.2
Weather forecast from Met. office for Europe (17/12/97)

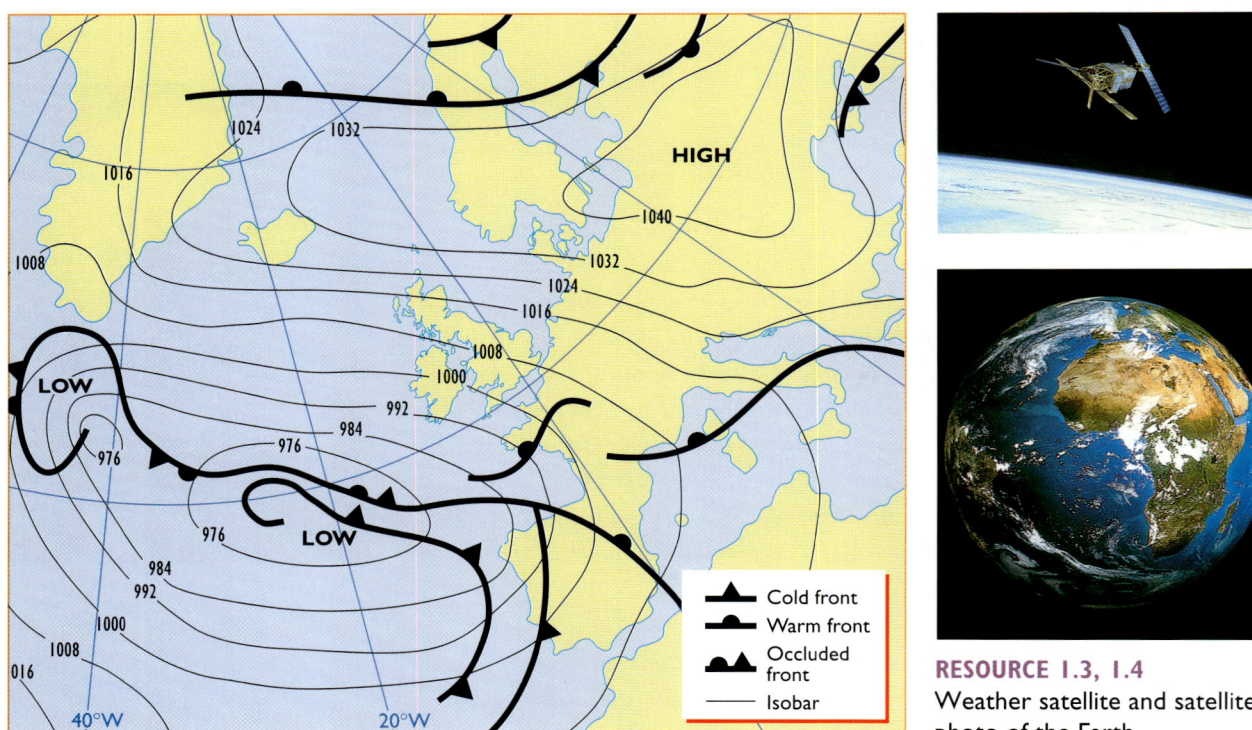

RESOURCE 1.3, 1.4
Weather satellite and satellite photo of the Earth

1. Using Resource 1.2, decide how the symbols on the weather map relate to the forecast.

2. Prepare your own weather forecast. What information do you need? Where would you find it? How reliable would that information be?

Weather – What Is It, and What Causes It?

Air masses

The weather of the British Isles is strongly influenced by the direction of the winds and where this movement of air is coming from. A pocket of air that spends some time over a particular area of land or sea, takes on the characteristics of that area. These pools of air are known as **'air masses'**. For example, air resting over the freezing continent of Europe in winter becomes very cold and dry. However, an easterly wind blowing this air over the North Sea can pick-up moisture and bring cold weather with snow showers to the East Coast. The meeting points between two air masses with different characteristics are called **'fronts'**. Just as hot and cold water in a bath do not mix immediately, so an air mass is slow to mix with another air mass when it moves from its 'source' area.

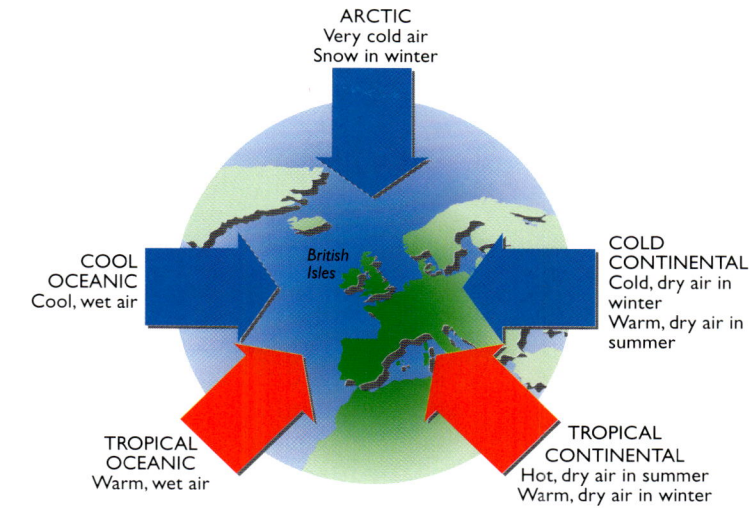

RESOURCE 1.5
Sources of air masses that converge on British Isles and their characteristics

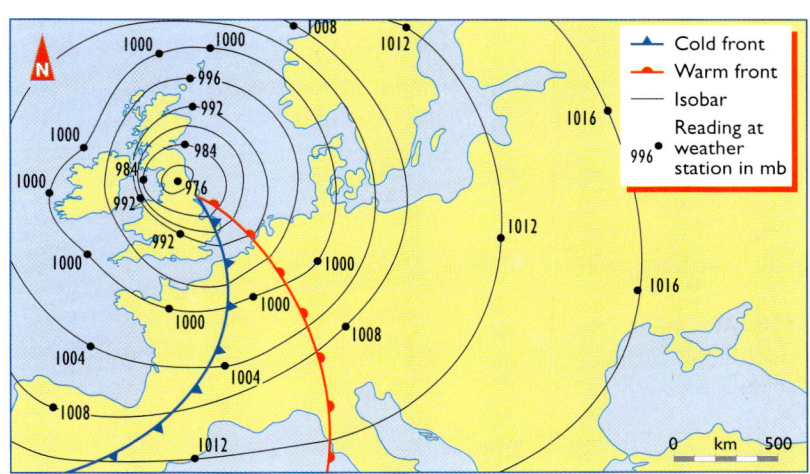

RESOURCE 1.6
UK Map with mb readings

Air pressure

This is one of the most important pieces of information gathered by weather forecasters. It is measured by a barometer in **millibars** (mbs), and is the weight of air pushing down on the Earth's surface. The curved lines that you see on a weather map are **isobars**. They join places with the same air pressure, and they are plotted at 4 millibar (4 mb) intervals. In a **low pressure** area or **'depression'** air is rising, and there is less weight of air pushing down on the surface. As air rises it expands, cools down, and condensation of water vapour takes place forming clouds. If a place is experiencing low pressure its weather is likely to be cloudy, possibly with rain, snow or hail.

On the other hand, in a **high pressure** area or **'anticyclone'**, the air is sinking towards the surface. As the air sinks it is compressed and warms up. As warm air can hold more water vapour than cold, any clouds 'disappear' as the water droplets evaporate and change back into water vapour. If an area is experiencing high pressure, then its weather is likely to be calm, settled and dry.

Wind always tries to blow from a 'high' to replace the rising air in a 'low'. However, if you look at the wind direction arrows shown on weather maps, you will notice that it is blowing almost parallel to the isobars. This is because the wind is deflected by the Earth turning on its axis. This causes the wind to travel on a curved track. In the northern hemisphere the flow is anti-clockwise around the 'Low', but to the south of the Equator it is clockwise.

The atmosphere

The **atmosphere** is a layer of air, about 50 kilometres thick, that surrounds our planet, Earth. It is a mixture of different kinds of gases, including varying amounts of water vapour. All of our weather takes place in the lower layers of the atmosphere up a to height of about 10 km. The air in this layer is always on the move as winds try to even out temperature differences between one part of the globe and another. The oceans are also major stores of heat, and ocean currents play an important part in the Earth's heat balance.

Air in contact with warm surfaces, both land and sea, is heated and rises creating a low pressure area. The warmest zone is around the Equator. Towards the Poles the air sinks back to the surface. Very fast moving winds found at heights of about 9 km, called **jet streams**, are part of this process. The jet streams along with differences in air pressure control the movement of winds at the Earth's surface.

The atmosphere contains water vapour (water in the form of an invisible gas), but the amount can vary from 0 up to 4%. The percentages of nitrogen, oxygen and 'other gases' are reduced accordingly. 'Other gases', totalling 1%, includes argon, carbon dioxide, and very tiny amounts of hydrogen, krypton, neon, helium and ozone.

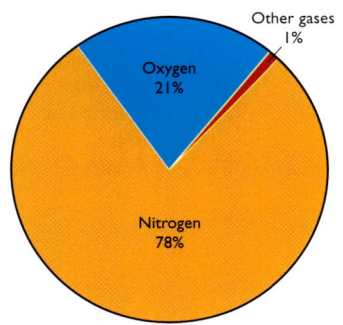

RESOURCE 1.7
Gases in the Earth's Atmosphere

3. What are millibars the measure of? What instrument do we use to measure millibars?

4. Define the following items, and explain why they are so important:
   - air masses
   - air pressure
   - atmosphere

5. a) How often are satellite pictures used in television weather forecasts?

   b) What aspects of the weather show up best on satellite pictures? Why do you think that is?

   c) Are satellite pictures as important as what the weather forecaster tells us? Explain your answer.

Weather – What Is It, and What Causes It?

Different types of weather

Each of the symbols below, and those used on the weather map (Resource 1.8) are used to indicate a form of weather. They act as a shorthand way to see how the weather is going to be at a certain time. When we see a cloud with a zig zag line emerging, we know there are going to be thunderstorms. When we see a cloud with three drops of water, we know this indicates rain. The symbols help us to quickly understand what is going on, but have you ever wondered why these things are going on?

RESOURCE 1.9
Wind symbol

RESOURCE 1.10
Rain symbol

RESOURCE 1.11
'Sun' symbol

RESOURCE 1.12
Thunder symbol

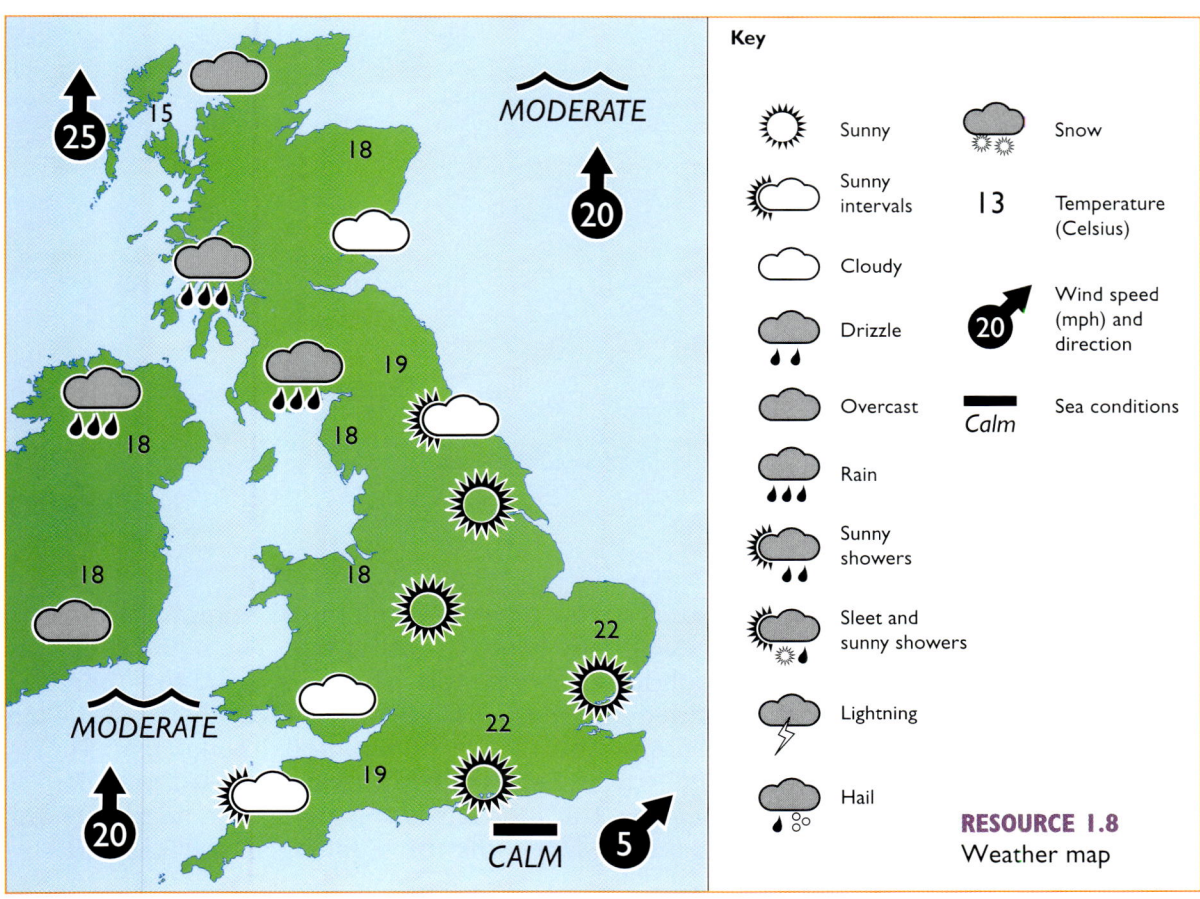

RESOURCE 1.8
Weather map

RAIN

Precipitation

Clouds are made of tiny, visible, water droplets or ice crystals, about 20 microns (0.02 mm) in diameter. A raindrop, however, is around 2,000 microns (2 mm). Rain, snow or hail falling from a cloud, is called **'precipitation'**. Various processes must take place which cause the water droplets or ice crystals to merge together, because precipitation only falls after the droplets or crystals have become large enough to overcome any rising air currents. Turbulence in the cloud makes droplets 'bump' into each other or, if there are ice crystals present, water droplets may stick to them.

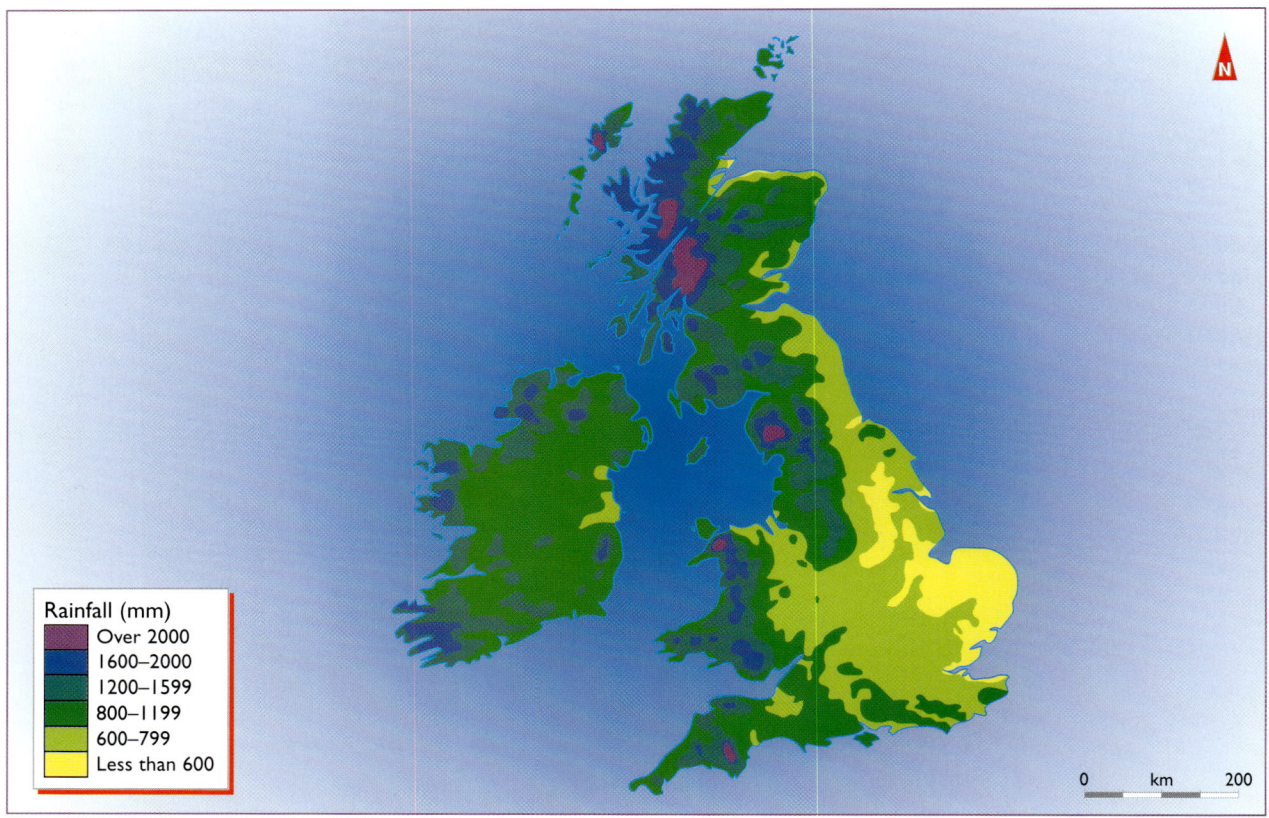

RESOURCE 1.13
Average rainfall distribution in the British Isles

If the air continues to rise after reaching the dewpoint, the temperature will eventually fall to 0° Centigrade. The liquid droplets then freeze and solidify as ice crystals. They may bond together, forming small 6-sided **snowflakes**. Often, many individual flakes cling together as large floppy snowflakes, heavy enough to fall from the cloud. If, as it usually is, the air temperature at the bottom of the cloud is above freezing, the snowflakes will melt – rain nearly always begins as snowflakes! **Sleet** is a mixture of falling snowflakes and raindrops.

Weather – What Is It, and What Causes It?

Blizzards are heavy falls of snow driven by a strong wind. The snow blows into hollows and is trapped by obstacles forming snow drifts. Described as a 'whiteout', it can be very difficult to see through the whirling snowflakes, making journeys extremely dangerous in blizzard conditions, especially in hilly districts. They bring chaos to travellers as roads are blocked, air traffic is diverted and trains get stuck.

RESOURCE 1.14
Motorists dig out cars on snowy day

What are the effects on temperature of distance from the sea?

How far a place is from the sea effects its temperature, although the impact of this influence varies between summer and winter. In winter, places far inland cannot benefit from the sea's warming effects. In summer, however, onshore winds keep seaside places cooler. Moscow and Edinburgh are the same distance from the Equator, 56° N, but compare their average summer and winter temperatures. The further inland a place is, the larger the differences between summer and winter temperatures will be – very cold in winter, but hot in summer. The interiors of continents are said to have **Continental Climates**.

	Moscow	Edinburgh
6. January average temperature	−17° C	+3° C
July average temperature:	+19° C	+14° C

Find Moscow and Edinburgh in your Atlas. Edinburgh is located by the sea on the Firth of Forth. Using the scale of the map, how many kilometres is Moscow from the nearest area of sea?

What is the difference between the July and January average temperatures in **a)** Moscow? **b)** Edinburgh. Why is there this difference?

Hodder Geography – Weather, Climate & Ecosystems

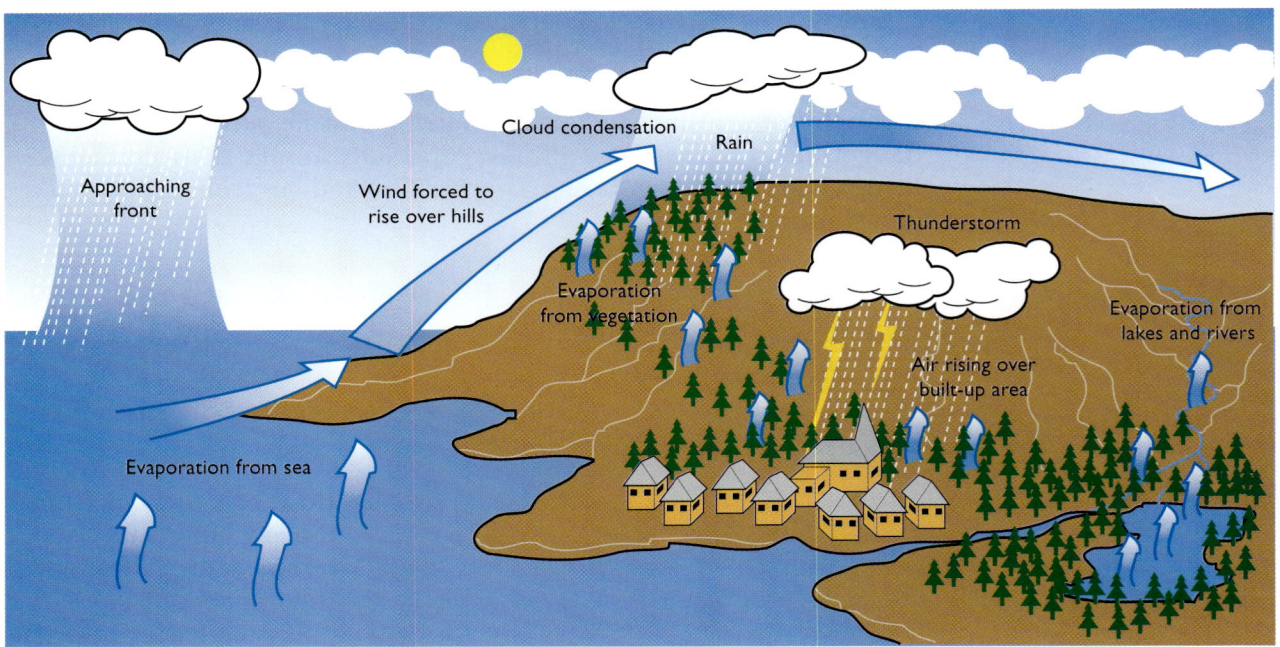

RESOURCE 1.15
Some rain-forming processes

7. Using an Atlas and Resources 1.13–1.18, explain which parts of Britain are
   a) the highest?
   b) the lowest?
   c) the wettest?
   d) the driest?

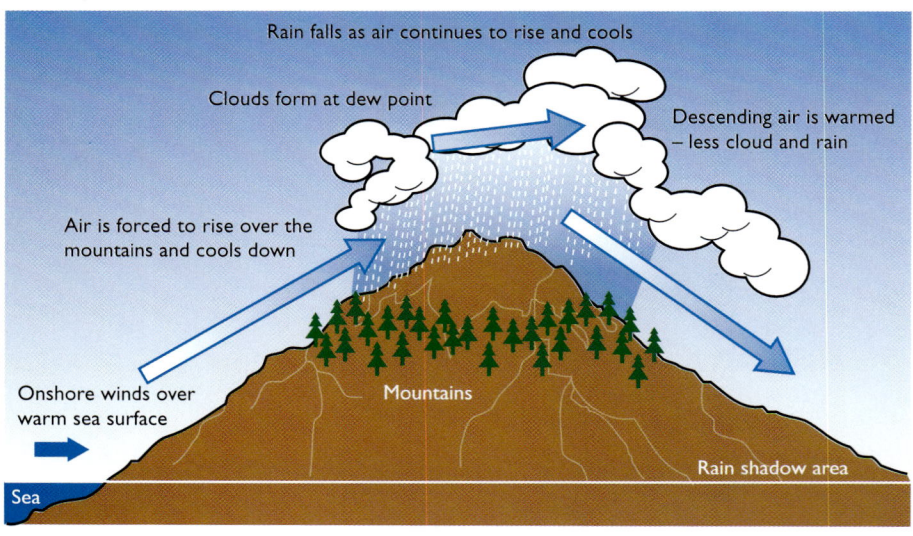

RESOURCE 1.16
How 'relief' or 'mountain' rain is formed

Weather – What Is It, and What Causes It?

Effects of high land on rainfall

In the British Isles it is much more hilly in the west of the country. As we get more winds blowing from the west than any other direction this, combined with the higher land, means that the west is wetter than the east.

When air blows towards a hill or mountain it is forced to rise over this barrier in its path. As it does so the air cools and water vapour condenses. If it rises high enough, rain or snow will fall on the mountains. This is known as 'relief' or 'mountain rain'. Once beyond the line of hills the air descends and warms up again. Because of this, places sheltered by mountains often receive less rainfall and are said to be 'rain shadow areas'.

RESOURCE 1.17
Mt. Fuji

TEMPERATURE

Effects of high land on temperature?

Mount Kilimanjaro in Tanzania rises to 5,895 metres above sea level. Although it is located on the Equator, it is snow covered all the year round due to its great height. As he climbed Kilimanjaro, a mountaineer reported these temperatures:

Height
Temperature
2,000 metres   +20° C
3,500 metres   +5° C
4,000 metres   0° C
5,000 metres   −10° C

8. What was the difference in temperature between 2,000 and 5,000 metres?

9. What height was the mountaineer when the temperature fell to freezing point?

10. How much does the temperature drop for every 100 metres of height gained?

11. Llanberis is a village at the foot of Mt. Snowdon in North Wales (85 metres above sea level). On 25 April the air temperature in Llanberis was 15° C. Some climbers called at the local tourist office to ask what the temperature would be at the top of Snowdon (1,085 metres above sea level). Although there is no weather station on Snowdon they were given the right answer. What were they told? (NB. Use your knowledge from the answer to question 10!)

12. Describe 3 ways in which heavy snowfall and blizzards can create hazards for people in mountainous areas.

Avalanches are a particular hazard after blizzards in high mountainous areas such as the Alps. An avalanche is a huge mass of snow, ice and rock which, without warning, cascades down a steep slope. This can occur when there is a slight thaw or after a build-up of new, heavy snow on top of old. An avalanche may be triggered by loud noises or other vibrations, and are a particular problem for skiers who could be buried as the avalanche smothers everything in its path.

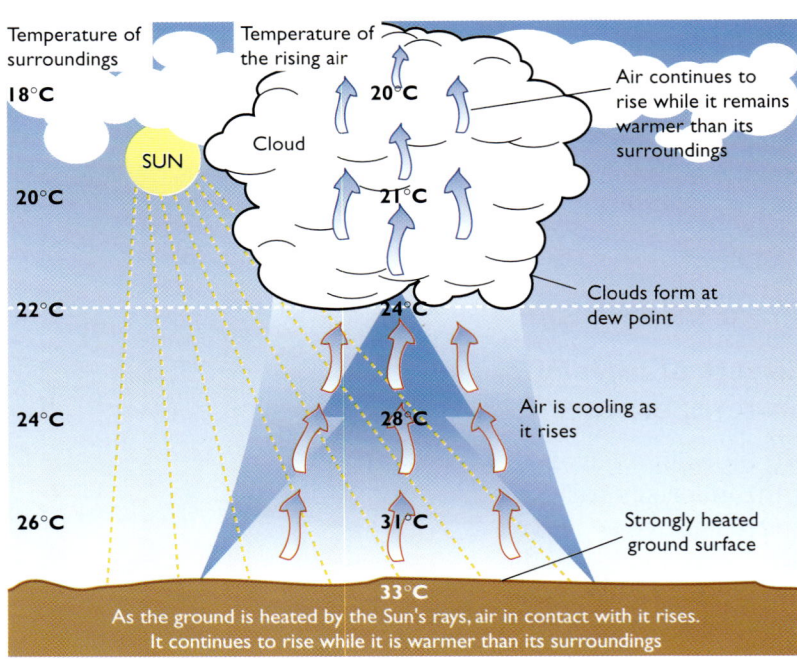

RESOURCE 1.18
How convectional rain is formed

Convectional rain

The Earth's surface heats up very unevenly. Concrete, tarmac and soil heat more quickly than areas of water or land covered by crops or forest creating '**hot spots**'. Air in contact with a hot spot is heated and rises like a huge bubble. The rising air can trigger-off heavy storms called '**convectional rain**'.

RESOURCE 1.19
Lightning over Tampa Bay, Florida, USA

Thunderstorms

At this very moment someone, somewhere, is experiencing a thunderstorm. There are around 40,000 such storms in the world every day! For a thunderstorm to develop, the cloud must rise to about 10,000 metres – the height of Mount Everest! The top of the cloud is well below freezing point and a flat head of ice crystals appears, shaped like a blacksmith's anvil. This is a cumulonimbus cloud. Strong convection currents churn the raindrops around, sweeping them upwards in the cloud over and over again to form hailstones. When these are heavy enough they fall in a down-draught with torrential rain, causing local flooding.

RESOURCE 1.20
Aerial view of the anvil-shaped top, or thunderhead, of a cumulo nimbus storm cloud

Thunder and lightning

Turbulence in a cloud causes friction between ice pellets and droplets, and opposing electrical charges build up. The top of the cloud and the ground below become positively charged (+), but the cloud's base is negatively charged (−). These opposite charges are strongly attracted to each other, resulting in a huge, rapid, electrical discharge – a flash of lightning! In a fraction of a second the air is heated to over 20,000° C. It expands rapidly, and we hear a clap of thunder.

Hailstones

In a thunder-cloud violent updraughts repeatedly sweep raindrops high into the atmosphere, where they freeze as ice pellets. These get bigger and bigger as a layer of water freezes around them each time they go around. Eventually they become heavy enough to overcome the powerful air currents that have been holding them up in the cloud. Hailstones the size of a grapefruit and weighing as much as a kilogram have been recorded!

RESOURCE 1.21
Macro photograph of hailstones

13. What problems might a thunderstorm bring to:
    a) traffic on a motorway?
    b) someone living close to a river?
    c) a farmer growing cereal crops?
    d) a tall tree or building?

Low pressure systems

Some exceptionally low pressures can occur in tropical and sub-tropical areas, causing some very violent weather. Fortunately for the British Isles these conditions do not affect us very often. The so-called 'hurricane' that raged across southern Britain in 1987, was, in reality, only a very violent gale.

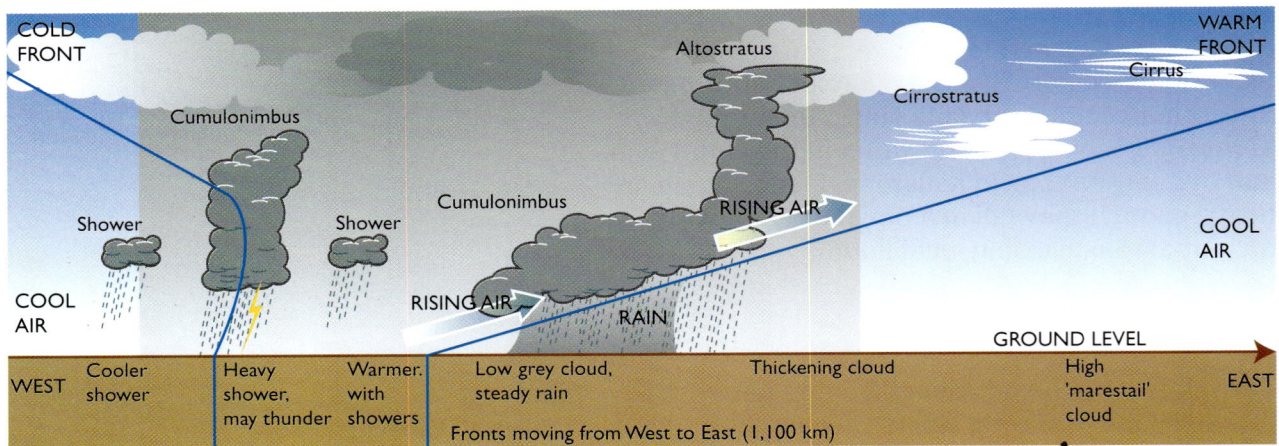

RESOURCE 1.22
Cross-section through a depression

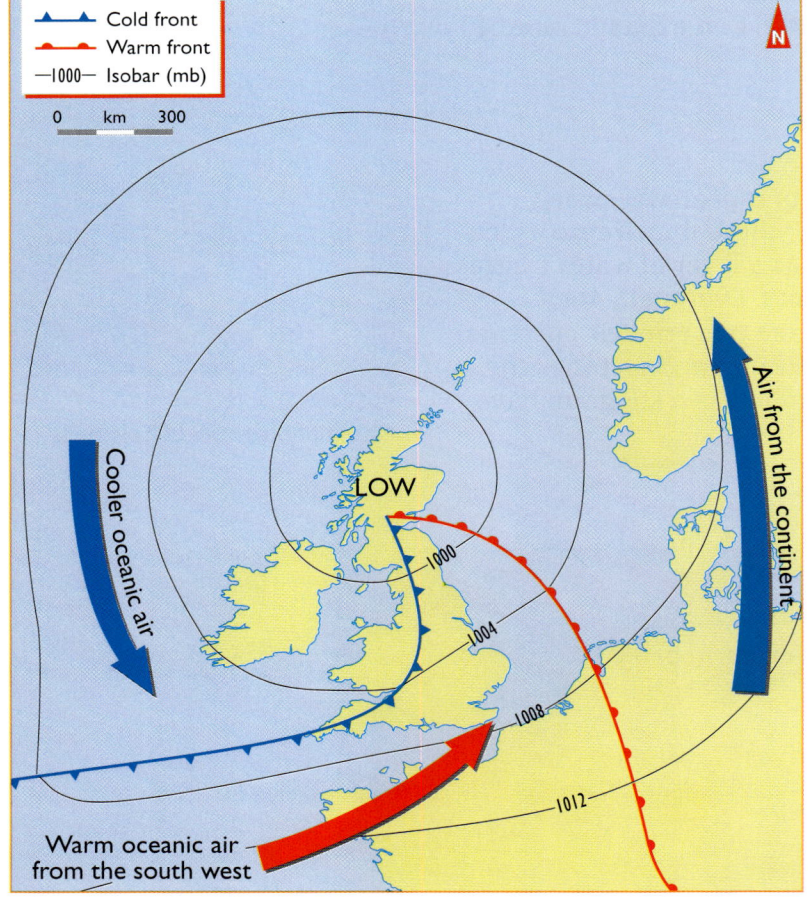

Frontal rain

When air in contact with the land is heated, it rises. So, there is less weight of air pushing down on the surface and is an area of **low pressure**. When air rises it expands and cools, and the water vapour in it condenses forming clouds. An area of low pressure rain is especially found along the 'fronts' – the junction of two different air masses, where cold air moving from the polar regions meets warm air from the tropics (See page 3). The warmer air rises along the line of the front, clouds form and rain may fall as a front passes overhead. Fronts are shown by particular symbols on weather maps.

RESOURCE 1.23
2 front depression

Hurricanes

There can be few weather systems as violent and terrifying as a hurricane! Called 'typhoons' in the Pacific, and 'tropical cyclones' in the Indian Ocean, these massive revolving tropical storms, as much as 1,000 kilometres across, bring ferocious winds reaching 250 kph, with gusts of over 300 kph. They particularly affect the Caribbean and south-east coast of the United States in August and September, when sea temperatures reach 27° C. In order to track them more easily each of these huge storms is given a male and female name alternately.

Hurricanes seldom travel beyond 30° N or S but, if they do, they decay to become a normal, if deep, low pressure area. A special feature is the **'eye'** at the hurricane's centre. This is a hole in the clouds, about 30 km across, with descending air. At the surface conditions are suddenly calm following the violent winds and torrential rain that have just been experienced. Around the eye a wall of cloud rises vertically into the atmosphere.

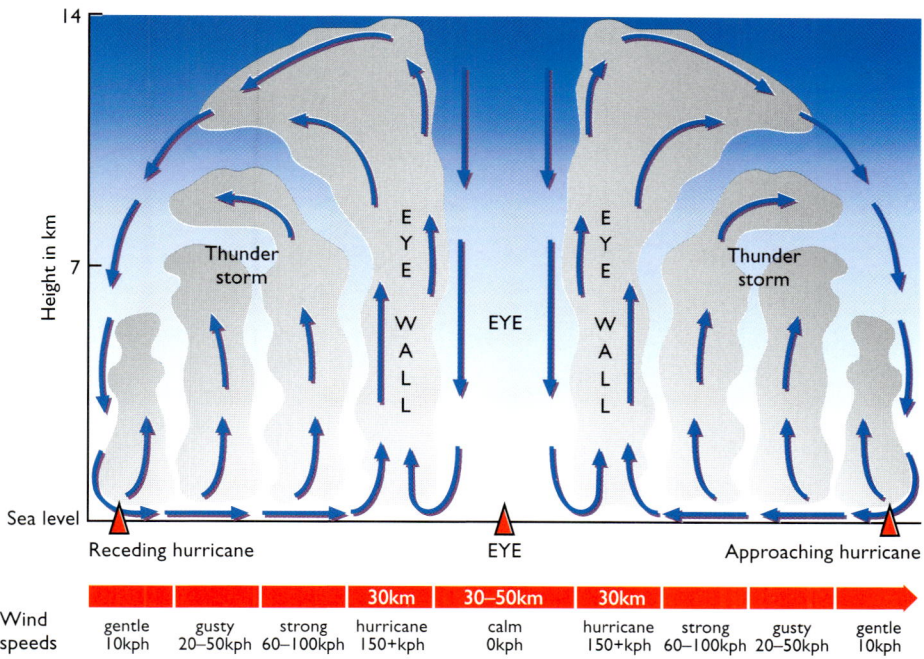

RESOURCE 1.24
Diagrammatic cross section of a hurricane

14. Explain why it may not be a very good idea to take a holiday in Florida or the West Indies in August and September.

15. What precautions would people need to take if a hurricane is forecast?

Spirals of cloud make it easy to identify hurricanes on satellite images. Their movements are carefully watched and places lying in the path of the storm can be given an early warning of the destruction and devastation that will follow.

The eye soon passes over, and the temporary calm is suddenly replaced by more deluges of rain and violent winds, but now blowing from the opposite direction.

RESOURCE 1.25
Destruction and havoc caused by Hurricane Hugo

16. What are the differences between the weather of a hurricane and a tornado?

17. Keep newspaper cuttings of reports about tornadoes and hurricanes and the devastation they cause.

18. What precautions would people need to take if a hurricane is forecast?

19. Why might insurance companies be concerned about insuring properties in south-east USA?

20. Using **Resource 1.26**, explain why a tornado is also called a 'twister'?

Tornadoes

Tornadoes or 'twisters' are extremely savage but compact storms. They are seldom more than 600 metres across, and are short lived. However, these 'whirl-winds' can cause very severe damage when they occur. They move fast and may suddenly change direction for no apparent reason. The damage is caused by wind speeds that can reach 400 km per hour – so powerful that yachts, cars and timber-built houses can be lifted high into the air! Even brick-built houses in a tornado's path may have their roofs ripped off. Tornadoes are quite common from the Gulf of Mexico to the Great Lakes in the USA – as many as 750 take place in most years. Oklahoma has been called 'the tornado capital of the world'! Even in Britain 50 or 60 'moderate' tornadoes occur each year, an example being one that hit the town of Selsey, Sussex, on 7 Jan, 1998.

Two other unusually severe weather features are caused by rising and rotating columns of air in conditions of extreme low pressure. Firstly 'water spouts', which resemble tornadoes, but which happen over a lake or the sea. The funnel of rotating air rises from the surface to cloud level. However, the water in the spout is not being sucked up by the rising air but is due to condensation of water vapour as very humid air is forced to rise. They are a severe hazard to fishing vessels and other small boats in their path.

RESOURCE 1.26
A tornado

Secondly, **'dust devils'**, which occur from time to time in deserts and arid areas. They are like a miniature tornado made visible by the dust picked up by the whirling wind. However, they are not nearly as powerful, although they may damage buildings and have been the cause of traffic accidents.

Hodder Geography – Weather, Climate & Ecosystems

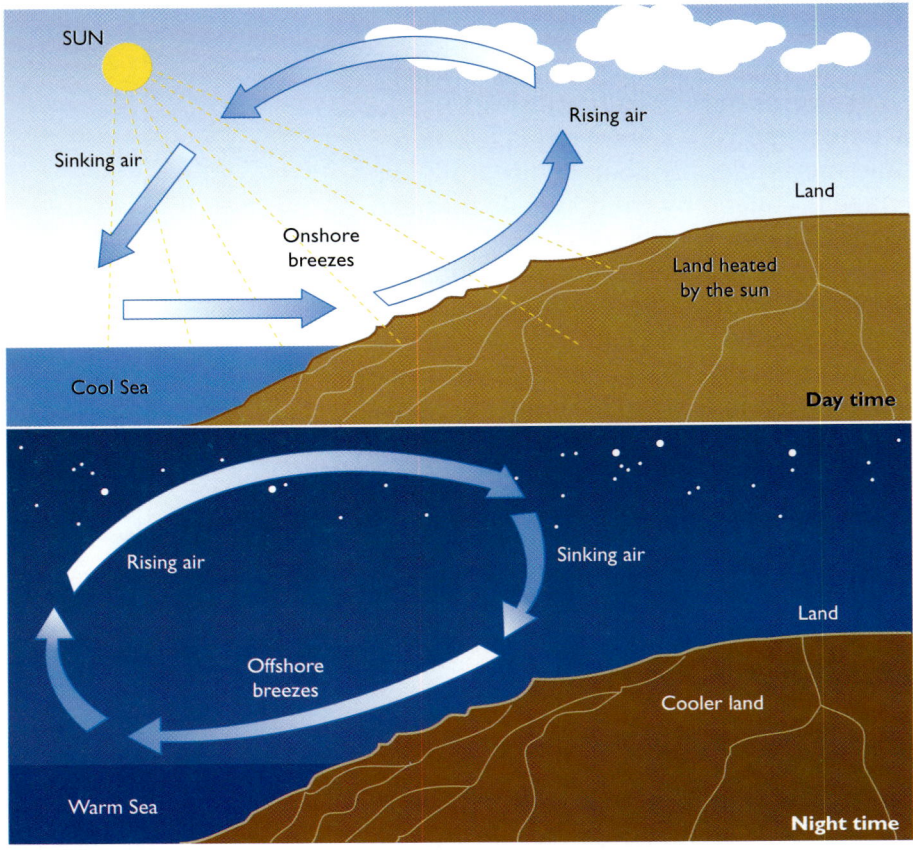

RESOURCE 1.27
Land and sea breezes

WIND

What makes the wind blow?

Different types of surface heat up at a different speeds. During daytime the land is warmed faster than the sea. The warm land heats the air above it which becomes lighter and rises, creating an area of local low pressure. Air is sucked in from over the sea to replace the rising air, and causes onshore sea breezes during daytime. At night the land cools faster than the sea and the wind direction is reversed, blowing in the opposite direction as a wind from land to sea.

Winds can be local or global. In the tropics large quantities of warm humid air rise creating an area of low air pressure in the Equatorial regions. The **Trade Winds** are caused by air blowing in to replace this rising air. 'Lows' also form nearer the Poles in the mid-latitudes, pulling in air to cause the **'Westerlies'** and **'Polar Easterlies'**. These are the 'depressions' that cause our changeable weather in the British Isles. Winds always blow from areas of high pressure to areas of low pressure. However, they are deflected by the rotation of the Earth and generally blow parallel to the isobars.

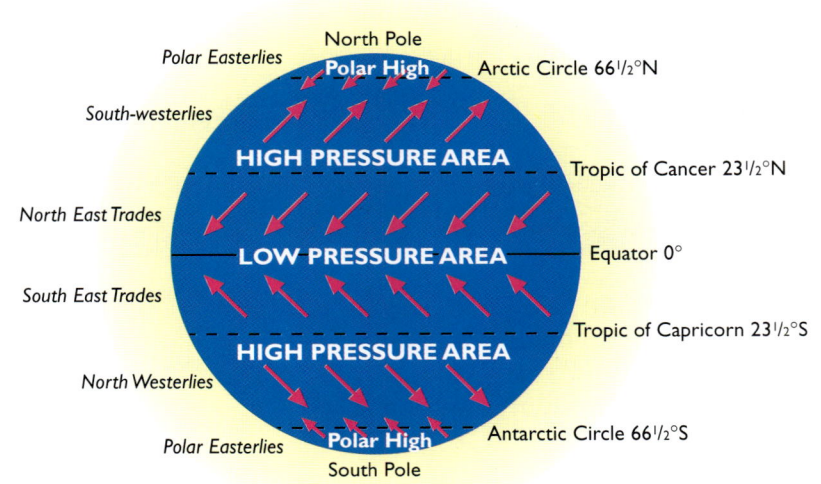

RESOURCE 1.28
Major wind belts of the Earth

The 'Wind-chill Factor' must be taken into account when temperatures are low and a strong wind is blowing. This causes a person to lose far more body heat than in still conditions. Exposed skin can freeze rapidly in the strong wind, causing frostbite and even death. In Canada and USA, freezing air can suddenly sweep southwards in winter, and warnings of possible wind-chill problems are given in forecasts.

21. What precautions might people take if a weather forecast warns of a strong risk from wind-chill?

High pressure systems

An area of high pressure, also called an **anticyclone**, usually brings dry weather with clear skies. This is an area where air is sinking in the atmosphere, and pressing down on the surface. As the air sinks it warms up and clouds evaporate. Unlike low pressure areas anticyclones are very slow moving, so the weather is likely to be settled for several days. However, the exact weather conditions will depend on the time of year and the time of day.

In the British Isles in summer, an anticyclone will usually give several days of calm, sunny, hot weather – the kind we would all like to have during the summer holidays!

In winter, however, an anticyclone can bring problems of frost, icy roads and fog, although there is little chance of rain or snow. At night it gets very cold at ground level due to the lack of cloud cover and, as the temperature falls, water vapour in the air condenses to give heavy dew, early morning mist and fog. If it falls below 0° C, frost and ice form. Later in the day these conditions will clear if the sun is warm enough to 'burn them off', but in mid-winter foggy, frosty conditions may last all day.

OTHER TYPES OF WEATHER

Mists and fogs

Mists and fogs are 'clouds at ground level'. They consist of billions of tiny water droplets suspended in the air. Fog is seldom more than 300 metres deep and usually only a few metres deep. They form during an anticyclone when there is no cloud cover. At night, temperatures fall and water vapour in the air condenses into visible droplets. However, fogs can also occur when warm, damp air blows over a cold surface, or when cold air blows across warm water. A haze may consist of very scattered suspended water droplets, but more often it is the result of smoke or other particles such as dust or industrial pollution suspended in the air.

	Fog	Mist	Haze
Visibility distance in metres	0 to 1,000	1,001 to 2,000	2,001 to 10,000

RESOURCE 1.29

Smog

'Smog' is short word for a 'smoke fog', but there are two types.

1. Before the Clean Air Acts of the 1950s, most power stations in Britain burned coal. Coal gas was also produced. Few homes had central heating, and most relied on smoky coal fires for winter warmth. In the cities the smoke from coal fires, fumes from industry and the exhaust from cars and lorries all mixed with the fog, turning it into a thick, yellow 'pea-souper'. These smogs lasted for several days, causing asthma, bronchitis and many other breathing problems. The Clean Air Acts banned coal burning in the cities and since then there have been fewer such smogs.

2. 'Smog' also describes the fog that forms under anticyclonic conditions in warm countries in large cities such as Los Angeles, Athens and Mumbai (Bombay) and even Paris and London during a hot summer's day. These cities have huge amounts of road traffic and, therefore, air pollution from exhaust fumes. The air sinking in the anticyclone traps these fumes and the bright sunlight causes a chemical reaction in the polluted air. This produces visible particles of hydrocarbons which are suspended in the air and ground-level ozone, a harmful gas, which damages plants. Both these pollutants cause stinging eyes, asthma and other breathing problems.

RESOURCE 1.30
Smog over Mumbai, a view from outside the city

Frosts

The story of the mythical Jack Frost, who was said to decorate window panes with feathery patterns of ice, came from Scandinavia where heavy frosts are very common in winter. In Britain we occasionally experience beautiful white hoar frosts, when temperatures fall below zero on clear nights during an anticyclone. Moisture in the air freezes onto every cold surface, coating them with a thick layer of sparkling ice crystals.

Frost damage

Occasional frosts can be a problem to farmers and fruit growers, especially in such places as California, Florida and Southern France, where oranges, lemons and grapefruit are grown. The ice crystals damage the buds of the fruit bushes, and this severely reduces the harvest later in the year. When night frosts are forecast in such places, drums of oil may be burned, placed under orchard trees to raise the air temperature. Elsewhere, fine jets of warm water may be sprayed onto the trees, and even helicopters have been hired to fly over the orchard throughout the night to keep the air moving and mix it with the heat from the helicopter's engine.

Frost can damage road surfaces as ice crystals expand when liquid water freezes beneath stones and in cracks, 'heaving' them apart. 'Black ice' is a particular hazard to motorists. A road surface may be wet, from melted snow or recent rain. When the temperature falls below freezing, it can become glazed over with ice. It is hard to see as it is the same colour as the damp surface, but is incredibly slippery.

RESOURCE 1.31
White hoar frost

22. Describe the main differences between a haze, a mist and a fog.
23. Why are frosts likely to occur in the British Isles when air pressure is high?

Climate

WHAT IS BRITAIN'S CLIMATE?

If the weather could be said to be what is happening out in the world at any given time, then the climate of a particular place could be explained as being the prevailing trend of the weather in that area. For example, Britain is described as having a 'cool temperate oceanic' climate. However, even within such a small area as Britain the climate is not all the same. The climate of the British Isles is strongly influenced by:

- Their location on the north-eastern side of the Atlantic Ocean;
- They are islands, therefore surrounded by sea;
- Their situation midway between the Tropics and the Poles in the 'mid-latitudes' – 50° to 60° North.

WHY IS IT HOT IN THE TROPICS BUT COLD AT THE POLES?

RESOURCE 1.32
Illustrating Sun's Rays

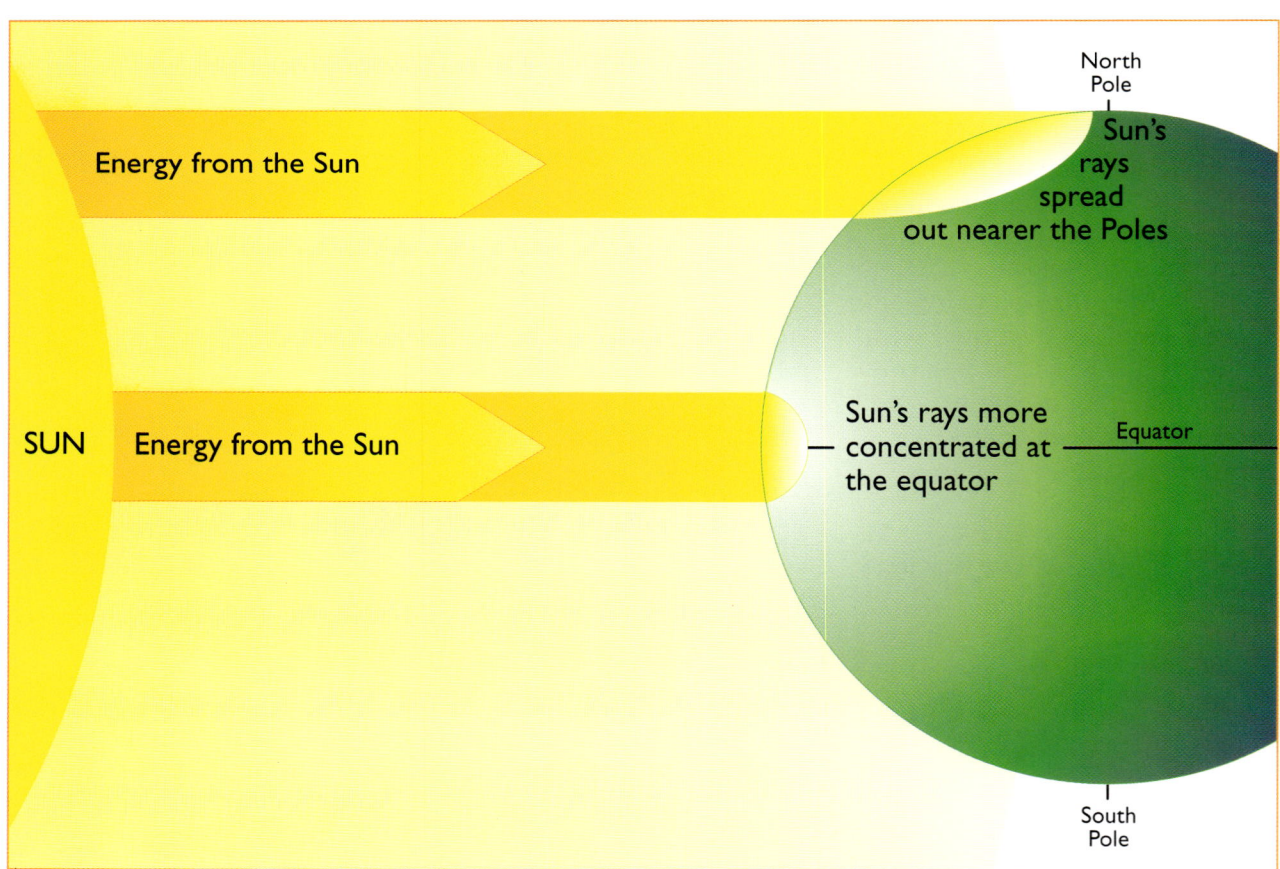

So far as the Earth is concerned, the Sun is like a gigantic 'radiator'. It supplies heat-energy to the Earth's surface which, in turn, warms the air in contact with the surface. However, due to the curved shape of the globe, this heat energy is not evenly spread. It is more spread out nearer the Poles, and so temperatures here are much lower than those at the Equator. The high temperatures around the Equator causes air to rise giving a zone of low pressure and much rainfall.

WHAT IS THE INFLUENCE OF CLIMATE?

The climate of a place has many effects on the people, plants and animals that live there. As far as we people are concerned, it effects the kinds of buildings we live in and the clothes we wear. Shorts and a 'T' shirt are great for a warm summer's day; but it would be very foolish to go out in such thin clothing when a blizzard is expected in winter!

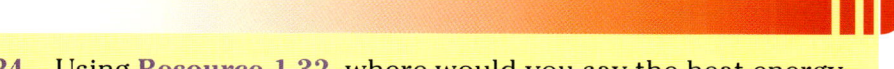

24. Using **Resource 1.32**, where would you say the heat energy from the sun is most concentrated – around the Equator or near the Poles? What would happen if that concentration changed?

25. Look again at **Resource 1.8**. Could you re-use the weather symbols to indicate the climate of a place on a world map? Would you need to make any new symbols?

2 MEASURING THE WEATHER

> ### Key Idea
> Measuring the weather might seem to be just another part of a weather forecast, but it is actually for more important than that: without daily records indicating how the weather changes, we wouldn't know how the weather works or why it behaves in the way it does.

Keeping weather records

If you have the necessary instruments you can keep a record of the weather from day to day, at home or at school. As we have seen, important aspects of the weather are: temperatures; amount of rainfall; air pressure; wind speed and direction; sunshine hours; amount of water vapour in the atmosphere. The particular records that you keep will depend on the instruments available to you.

Your school may have an 'automatic weather station' from which data is supplied to a computer and may be stored and processed on a disk. These records can make interesting comparisons from year to year, and it may be possible to detect slight differences in the climate over a small area.

Methods of measuring the weather

RESOURCE 2.1
A Stevenson's Screen used for the daily monitoring of weather conditions.

There are many different ways of measuring the weather. Here are just a few examples of the methods you could use to see what the weather is doing at any given time.

The weather figures opposite were collected at a school weather station like the one shown in **Resource 2.1**. The thermometers are kept in a Stevenson's Screen – a white painted box with slatted sides supported on a stand. Weather records should be collected every day. A recording sheet to keep a full week's records is very helpful.

MEASURING THE WEATHER

RESOURCE 2.2 A school/home weather recording sheet

Daily Weather Recordings for:							
(Name of school or person) (Place)							
Dates: .... to .... Month .... Year							
	Mon	Tue	Wed	Thu	Fri	Sat	Sun
Pressure (mbs)							
Maximum Temperature °C							
Minimum Temperature °C							
Rainfall mm							
Cloud cover (oktas)							
Cloud type							
Wind direction							
Wind force (kph or Beaufort Scale)							
Relative Humidity							

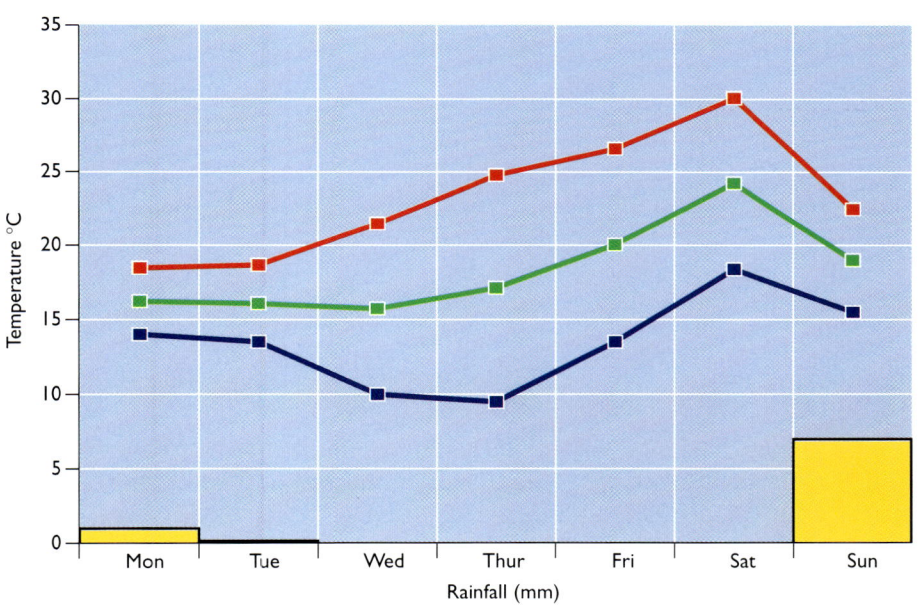

RESOURCE 2.3 Graph to show Max and Min Temperatures for a school in Cambridge

RESOURCE 2.4 Weather statistics for temperatures and rainfall recorded by a school in Cambridge for one week in July, 1996

Week 7–13 July 1996	Mon	Tue	Wed	Thu	Fri	Sat	Sun
Maximum Temperature °C	18.5	18.7	21.5	24.8	26.6	30.1	22.5
Minimum Temperature °C	14.0	13.5	10.0	9.5	13.5	18.4	15.5
Mean Temperature	16.25	16.1	15.75	17.15	20.05	24.25	19.0
Rainfall mm	2	trace	nil	nil	nil	nil	22
							Thunderstorm ↑

Measuring temperature

The highest (maximum) and lowest (minimum) temperatures in a 24 hour period can easily be recorded using a maximum and minimum thermometer. If you have not got access to a Stevenson's Screen make sure your thermometer is kept in the shade, as the temperature in the full sun will be much higher. Do not forget to reset the steel pins on the max–min thermometer each day with a magnet. Another useful figure is the Mean Temperature for the day or month. Mean Temperatures are found by adding the maximum and minimum temperatures and dividing by 2.

Rainfall

A rain gauge collects precipitation in a cylinder by means of a funnel. The amount collected is poured into a measuring cylinder and recorded in millimetres. A rain gauge should be placed in an open area away from buildings and trees.

You could try designing your own rain gauge using a bottle and a funnel, but remember that you will need to work out the relationship between the volume of rain collected and the area of the top of your funnel. You may need to ask your Geography or even your Maths teacher for some help!

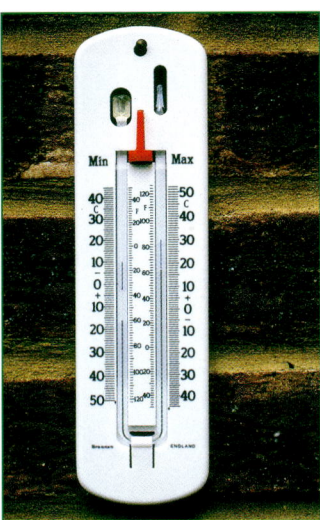

RESOURCE 2.5
A Max/Min thermometer

RESOURCE 2.6
A Rain Gauge

Study the weather data collected by a school in Cambridge shown in *Resources 2.3 and 2.4*.

1. What do you think is meant by the terms 'Maximum' and 'Minimum' Temperatures?

2. On which day did the greatest difference between 'Maximum' and 'Minimum' Temperatures occur?

3. Which day received the most rainfall, how much, and why?

4. Why is it an advantage to keep the thermometers in a Stevenson's Screen?

5. What are the maximum and minimum temperatures by the thermometer in *Resource 2.5*?

Measuring the Weather

Atmospheric pressure

This is measured by an instrument called a barometer, of which there are various types. The simplest consists of a glass tube filled with mercury standing in a trough. The tube is sealed at the top end. Air pressure holds the mercury at a particular height in the tube, this level rising or falling as the pressure changes. An aneroid barometer has a drum with a sensitive metal top which also responds to air pressure – you may have one hanging on the wall at home. It is fitted with an arrow and a gauge graduated in millibars. Barographs automatically record the pressure over 24 hours, tracing a line onto a cylindrical graph. Changes are easily seen. Does your school weather station have one?

Wind speed and direction

The *wind direction* can be noted from a weather vane. Is there one on your local church? Remember that wind direction is the direction *from* which the wind is blowing – a south-west wind blows *from* SW to NE. SW would be the direction to which the arrow will point as there is a weight on the arrow end.

Wind speed is measured by an anemometer. The cups spin around a spindle and a dial on the instrument gives a reading in km per hour. You can also observe wind speed by using the Beaufort Scale – see **Resource 2.8**.

RESOURCE 2.7
An anemometer

6. Keep a record of daily air pressure for a month. Plot the data on a graph joining the points to produce a line graph.

7. Keep a record of the wind direction and strength using the Beaufort Scale for the same month as for 6. Draw a 'wind rose' using your data. From which direction did the wind blow most frequently? Did the wind blow most strongly on days when pressure was low or high?

Force	Speed (kph)	Description	Indicators
0	Less than 1	Calm	Smoke rises in straight column
1	1–5	Light air	Smoke drifts slowly
2	6–11	Light breeze	Leaves rustle; wind vane turns
3	12–19	Gentle breeze	Leaves and smaller twigs move
4	20–29	Moderate breeze	Small branches move; dust blows about
5	30–38	Fresh breeze	Small trees sway
6	39–51	Strong breeze	Large branches sway; overhead wires 'whistle'
7	52–61	Near gale	Trees sway; it is hard to walk
8	62–74	Gale	Twigs snap off trees
9	75–86	Strong gale	Branches break; minor damage to buildings
10	87–101	Whole gale	Trees uprooted; significant damage to buildings
11	102–120	Storm	Widespread damage
12	Over 120	Hurricane	Widespread serious destruction

RESOURCE 2.8
The Beaufort Scale of Wind Speeds

DISPLAYING YOUR WEATHER RECORDS

From your studies of **Resources 2.2, 2.3 and 2.4** you will have noticed how much easier it is to understand the data if it is displayed 'visually' or 'graphically' so as to show variations and trends. Rainfall is always plotted on as a bar or 'chimney' graph, while temperature is shown as a line graph – see **Resource 2.4** which shows the data for each month of the year. The 'Mean Monthly Temperature' is calculated by adding up all the daily mean temperatures for that month and dividing by the number of days in the month.

8. What instrument is used to measure atmospheric pressure?

9. Which is most likely to produce fine weather – high or low pressure?

10. Using the Beaufort Scale, what would show you that the wind speed is around 50 kph?

11. Keep a record of maximum and minimum temperatures, rainfall, air pressure, wind direction and strength (using the Beaufort Scale) for one month. When the data has been collected, display your findings using appropriate graphs and diagrams as described in the next section. These might be drawn up using a computer or drawn on graph paper.

Cloud cover and type

In the limited space of this book it is not possible to describe all the different cloud types. You will need to refer to a more detailed book for photos of others. However, you can estimate the amount of cloud cover. You should estimate how much of the sky is covered with cloud to the nearest eighth, $\frac{1}{8}$ = 1 okta. If its half covered in cloud it is said to be $\frac{4}{8}$ or 4 oktas; if completely overcast it is $\frac{8}{8}$ = 8 oktas.

RESOURCE 2.9A
Clouds over Amazon River

RESOURCE 2.9B
An aerial view of Altocumulus cloud

Other measurements

Although not practical for home use, as the instruments are too expensive, school weather stations may have a hygrometer – a thermometer with a wet and dry bulb. This measures relative humidity – the amount of water vapour in the air.

Another expensive instrument is a sunshine recorder in which a glass sphere focuses the sun's rays onto a heat sensitive card. When the sun shines it burns a trace on the card which is marked out in hours, so that the total for the day can be assessed.

RESOURCE 2.10
A Sunshine recorder

Wind direction

Figures collected for wind direction are usually shown by plotting a 'wind rose'. The figures below were collected by a school in Cambridge for July 1992.

Wind direction	Calm	N	NE	E	SE	S	SW	W	NW
No. of Days	1	4	3	3	3	2	10	2	3

RESOURCE 2.11
Wind Direction, recorded by a Cambridge School for July 1992 and plotted on a wind rose

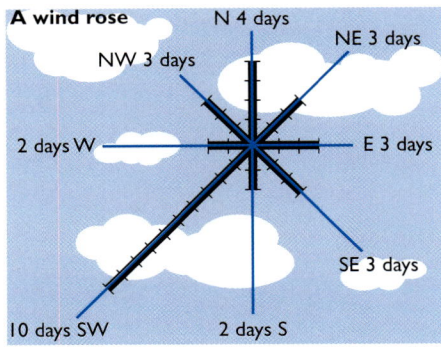

On a 'wind rose' the more days on which the wind blew in a particular direction, the longer the direction arrow will be.

RESOURCE 2.12
Monthly Rainfall Figures Recorded by a Cambridge School

Jan	Feb	Mar	Apr	May	Jun	Jul	Aug	Sep	Oct	Nov	Dec
49	08	54	40	49	30	80	82	53	75	82	32

Rainfall in millimetres. Total Rainfall for Year = 634 mm

12. The figures above are the amounts of rainfall recorded month by month during a year by a Cambridge School. Using graph paper ruled in millimetres plot these rainfall figures as a chimney graph. Your vertical scale can be 1 mm = 1 mm. Allow 1 cm of column for each month.

RESOURCE 2.13
Monthly Mean Temperature Figures Recorded by a Cambridge School

Jan	Feb	Mar	Apr	May	Jun	Jul	Aug	Sep	Oct	Nov	Dec
6.3	9.0	10.9	13.2	19.6	21.3	21.5	20.9	18.0	11.3	10.7	6.3

Temperatures in ° Centigrade

13. The figures above are the mean temperature figures recorded month by month for the same school. Above the rainfall graph on your graph paper, plot the mean monthly temperatures as a line graph.
Use a vertical scale of 1 mm = 1° Centigrade and position the dot in the middle of the 1 cm column allocated to each month.

MEASURING THE WEATHER

Microclimates

It has been said that our heads exist in a different climate from our feet! There can be quite marked variations in climate over a very small distance. These local contrasts are known as microclimates. It is quite easy to see small differences in climate around your home or school buildings. You will have noticed how in some spots frost lingers longer on a cold day, and how some places are sheltered from the wind, while others are very draughty.

On a larger scale the climate in our built-up areas has become rather different from the countryside round about (Resource 2.14).

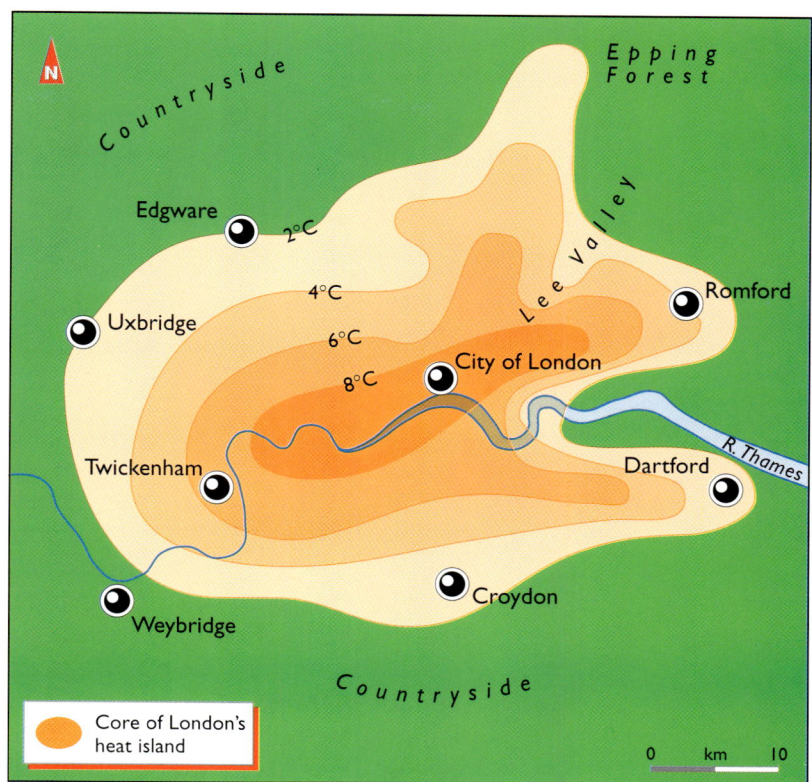

RESOURCE 2.14
Diagram to show London's Heat Island

14. What are the outdoor temperature differences around your school or home at a particular time? Use a thermometer to find out the outdoor temperature differences between a sunny and a shady spot.

15. Do buildings deflect the wind? Are some spots sheltered while others are draughty? Find out about air flow around buildings by tracking the path of bubbles made by blowing into a plastic or wire loop dipped into soapy water.

16. What are the wind speeds around the school site? If your school has a hand-held anemometer use it to discover where the windiest corners with the highest windspeeds are. Where is the most sheltered area of your school's grounds?

17. During frosty weather, map areas of the school grounds where frost lasts all day.

If you have carried out some of the investigations in the activity above, you will have a good idea of some of the factors causing microclimates around your school. These will include shelter by plants and buildings; their height; whether or not a place is shaded from the sun.

18. Look at the map (Resource 2.14). What is the temperature difference between the City of London and the countryside north of Edgware?

19. These warmer city areas are called 'heat islands'. As they act as 'hot spots' they cause bubbles of air to rise. As a result, are cities likely to experience *more* or *less* cloud and rain than the countryside around them?

Why do city heat islands occur?

As we have seen, temperatures in the centre of a city like London are up to 6° C higher than the country, especially at night. This happens partly because brick, stone and other building materials absorb heat from the Sun during the day. At night this is released slowly as if the building were a giant storage heater. City centres are also warmer because buildings are centrally heated, and even in summer air conditioning that cools the insides of shops and offices is pumping heat to the outside. In addition, car, lorry and bus engines release heat and cause smog. The heat and the pollution is trapped between tall buildings.

RESOURCE 2.15
New York, victim of both heat islands and wind tunnels

MEASURING THE WEATHER

Windy cities

Although pockets of warm air tend to be trapped by the city's buildings, helping to cause the heat island effect, cities can be very gusty places on windy days.

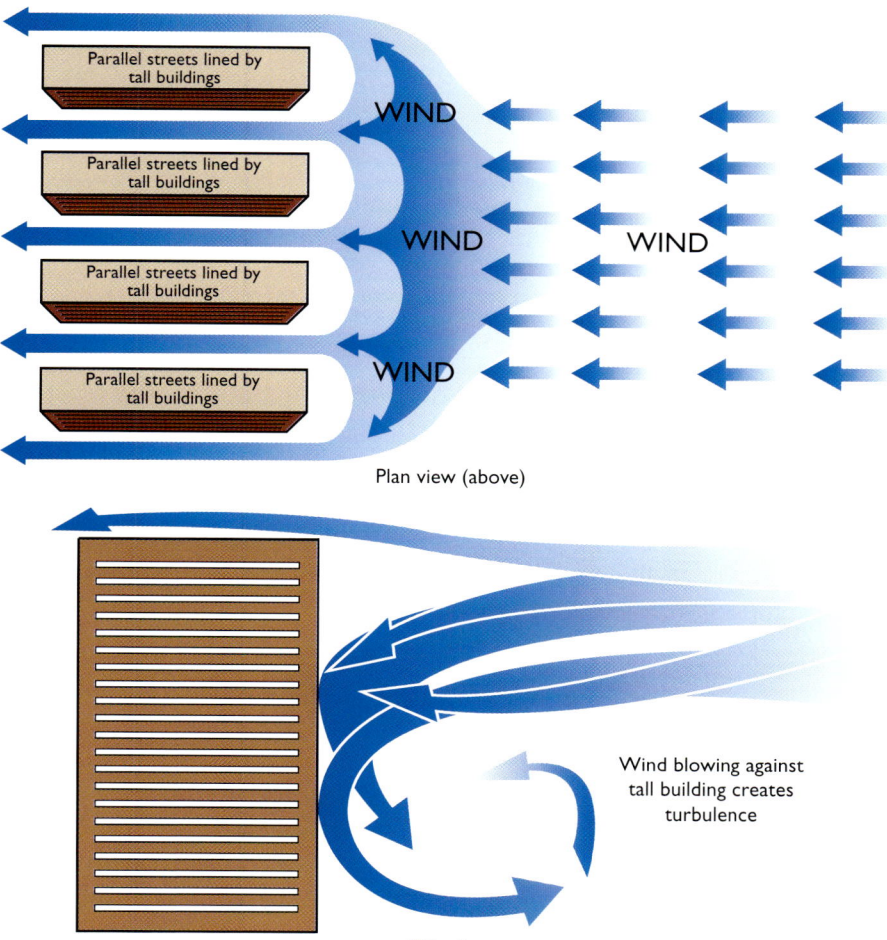

RESOURCE 2.16
Wind funnel effect

20. Look at the diagram in Resource 2.16. What is the effect of rows of tall buildings on the flow of air between them?

21. Although some cities receive a little more rain than the surrounding country areas, the air in cities is drier than air in the countryside. Explain two possible reasons for this.

22. What will happen to the rain that falls on the tarmac and concrete surfaces of built up areas? How might this explain why streams and rivers in cities are more likely to flood than those in the countryside?

ECOSYSTEMS

Key Idea

Ecosystems are enclosed systems made up of living and non-living matter. The ecosystem relies upon the relationships between the living and non-living matter to survive. When an individual part of an ecosystem is threatened, it can spell disaster for the ecosystem as a whole. This chapter will take a look at ecosystems, and the problems they can sometimes face.

What is an ecosystem?

Plants and animals cannot change their clothing, but during their evolution over millions of years they have developed many features that help them to survive in particular types of climate. Depending on where they live they may need to survive long periods of drought, wet seasons, cold winters or hot summers. These particular features are called 'adaptations'.

Over many millions of years plants and animals have evolved special adaptations that suit them to live in certain types of climate and to follow particular ways of life. We tend to group them together as living communities called 'ecosystems'. All the things that live in a natural ecosystem depend on each other for food, shelter and other parts of their lives.

RESOURCE 3.1
Polar bears live in the Arctic. How are they adapted to survive in snow and ice?

ECOSYSTEMS

There are two main parts to an ecosystem – the living and the non-living. **The non-living part** is the physical environment – the climate, water supply, type of soil and air. All these influence the things that can live in a particular place as they provide plants and animals with their essential needs – water, minerals, oxygen, carbon dioxide and living space. Climate is very important too. It affects the length of the growing season, the amount of moisture available and whether or not there are frosts and droughts that the living things must be able to survive. **The living part** is all the plants and animals that live together in an area forming a web of life. Some are **herbivores** which eat grasses or other plants – rabbits are a good example. Others are **carnivores** – the meat-eaters – living either as **predators**, who live on what they themselves kill and eat, or scavengers, who survive by consuming what the predators leave behind.

RESOURCE 3.2
Ecosystem in a typical piece of British Countryside

There is also another vital group of living organisms that might be described as 'nature's dustmen' – the **decomposers**. A fallen leaf, for example, becomes food for a host of earthworms, woodlice, fungi, bacteria and others that cause it to decay and return the vital minerals and nutrients of which it is made to the soil. A hectare of soil may contain as much as 10 tonnes of these organisms! In this chapter, we will be looking at three ecosystems, one within the British Isles and two in the larger world. As you read through each case study, think about how each ecosystem is similar, and how each is different.

Look at the picture of the ecosystem above. Make two lists:

1. **a)** of the non-living parts, and

   b) the living parts. By each item in this list say whether you think it is a herbivore (plant eater); a carnivore (meat-eater); food producer (plant); a scavenger, or a decomposer.

Coastal sand dunes

Sand dunes by the sea are a very specialised ecosystem found in the British Isles. At low tide, large areas of sand may be exposed. On warm days the surface dries and the sand is whipped across the beach by the wind which blows mainly from the south-west. At the head of the beach the wind blown sand is trapped by rubbish, stones and plants, piling up in large heaps called 'dunes'. East Head at West Wittering near the mouth of Chichester Harbour is a good example.

The dunes facing the sea are made of sand that has only recently been blown there, but a highly specialised plant is growing in it – marram grass. This grass is specially adapted to the dune conditions where water can be hard to get at. It has a rolled leaf, and the stomata (the cells in the leaf through which the leaf loses water) are on the inside of this tube. On a warm, dry day the leaves stay tightly rolled and marram grass is able to save the water that would otherwise evaporate. It also has an extremely long network of roots that binds the loose sand together. There is little proper soil in the newly formed dunes. The surface of the sand looks clean and so these are called **'yellow dunes'**.

When the marram grass dies, the dead leaves and roots start to form a thin soil on the sand in which other plants can grow. As you get further away from the sea more and more kinds of plants are found growing in the dunes. Among these are sea holly, sand spurge and different kinds of grasses and sedges. The thin soil on the sand looks 'dirty' and so here they are called **'grey dunes'**.

2. Sand dunes are formed from wind blown sand. Give *two* reasons why it is nearly always windy by the sea.

3. What problems must plants overcome if they are to live on a sand dune?

4. Name a specialist sand dune plant and describe its adaptations. Why do plants that live in sand dunes need special adaptations?

5. Why does the sand in the dunes change colour as the dunes get older?

6. Describe some of the methods used to stop dunes from being eroded.

7. Why has an area of salt marsh formed behind the dunes?

East Head is a very popular spot with holiday-makers who like to sunbathe and picnic in the dunes and to watch the birds, yachts and windsurfers using Chichester Harbour. Children like to play in the dunes. Unfortunately all these activities wear away the vegetation and the loose sand below is exposed to the wind and the rain. Erosion takes place and large hollows or 'blow-outs' appear as the wind carries the sand away. In places the dunes need to be fenced to stop people trampling and to prevent further erosion. The National Trust who look after the dunes have constructed board walks for people wishing to walk across them and planted more marram grass to bind the sand.

Behind the dunes at East Head lies an arm of Chichester Harbour that has been cut off from the main estuary by the growth of the dunes. The dunes shelter the water from the south-west winds, and mud and silt is deposited in the calm water. This has created an area of salt marsh. In winter, the marsh is used as a feeding area by hundreds of wading birds that probe in the mud for worms and shellfish and by brent geese that graze on the plants.

Strand line	Fore dunes	Yellow dunes	Grey dunes	Slack	Grey dunes	Salt marsh
Normal High Tide Mark	Affected by highest tides only	Constant supply of wind-blown sand	More humus more stable soil, so more plants can grow	Damp area – water-table at the surface	Similar to other grey dune area	Sheltered, calm water with salt-marsh
	Sea lyme grass	Sea lume and marram grass sea holly	Sand fescue grass, hawkbit	Reeds and small willows		Cord grass and sea-lavender

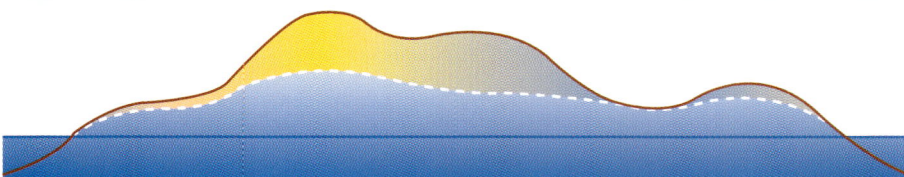

RESOURCE 3.3A
Cross section through dunes at East Head

RESOURCE 3.3B
Aerial shot of East Head

HODDER GEOGRAPHY - Weather, Climate & Ecosystems

What is it like in a rainforest?

'The majority of . . . creatures live in a part of the jungle that, until recently, was largely beyond our reach, . . . the canopy of leaves 50 metres above the ground.

Arriving there is like leaving the dim airless staircase of a tower block and emerging onto its roof. Suddenly the humid twilight is replaced by fresh air and sunshine. . . .

The canopy itself, the ceiling of the jungle, is a dense continuous layer of greenery some 6 or 7 metres deep. The leaves are protected with glossy waxy surfaces on which moss and algae would have great difficulty in getting a hold. Furthermore, nearly all the leaves have drip tips, elegant spikes at their ends like tiny spouts, which ensure that after a rain storm water does not linger but swills swiftly away, so keeping the top of the leaf well washed and dry. . . .

Here and there standing 10 metres or more above all the rest, rises a single isolated giant tree.'

RESOURCE 3.4
Description of tropical forest by David Attenborough, 'The Living Planet'. BBC/Collins 1984

RESOURCE 3.5
Tropical rainforest tree with buttress roots. Note how dark it is on the forest floor

Many films set in rainforests give a false impression of what they are like. Their images often suggest a thick undergrowth through which travellers must hack a path with a machete. While this may be true of forest margins – e.g. by a river where there is more light – over most of the forest floor there is plenty of space to move about. The light here is too dim for undergrowth to grow. It is only when an old tree dies that a shaft of light can penetrate the shady gloom, saplings burst into life and struggle upwards in a desperate competition to get to the sunlight. Many trees have buttress roots to support their great height. Orchids, ferns and creepers (lianas) grow from their branches and from crevices in tree trunks.

RESOURCE 3.6
Climate figures for Singapore (1° N, 10 m above sea level)

Climate figures for Singapore (1° N, 10 m above sea level)

Month	Jan	Feb	Mar	Apr	May	Jun	Jul	Aug	Sep	Oct	Nov	Dec
Temperature °C	26	27	27	27	28	27	27	27	27	27	27	27
Rainfall mm	251	173	193	188	173	173	170	196	178	208	254	257

Total = 2414 mm

8. Singapore is in south-east Asia. Its climate supports a tropical rainforest ecosystem. Similar figures would be found for other parts of Malaysia and Indonesia. Draw a graph to show these figures.

9. Explain why this climate is ideal for the growth of tropical rainforests.

Places with tropical rainforest have a climate with heavy rainfall throughout the year and high temperatures, averaging 27° C. There are no true seasons. These conditions are ideal for plant growth. Rainforests are extremely rich habitats for wildlife and are home to more than a half of all the Earth's living species. More varieties of plants are found in tropical rainforests than in any other ecosystem. Most of the wildlife lives in the treetops – the canopy layer where there is sunshine and fresh air. Many kinds of monkeys, brightly coloured birds, reptiles and even frogs are found living high in the trees.

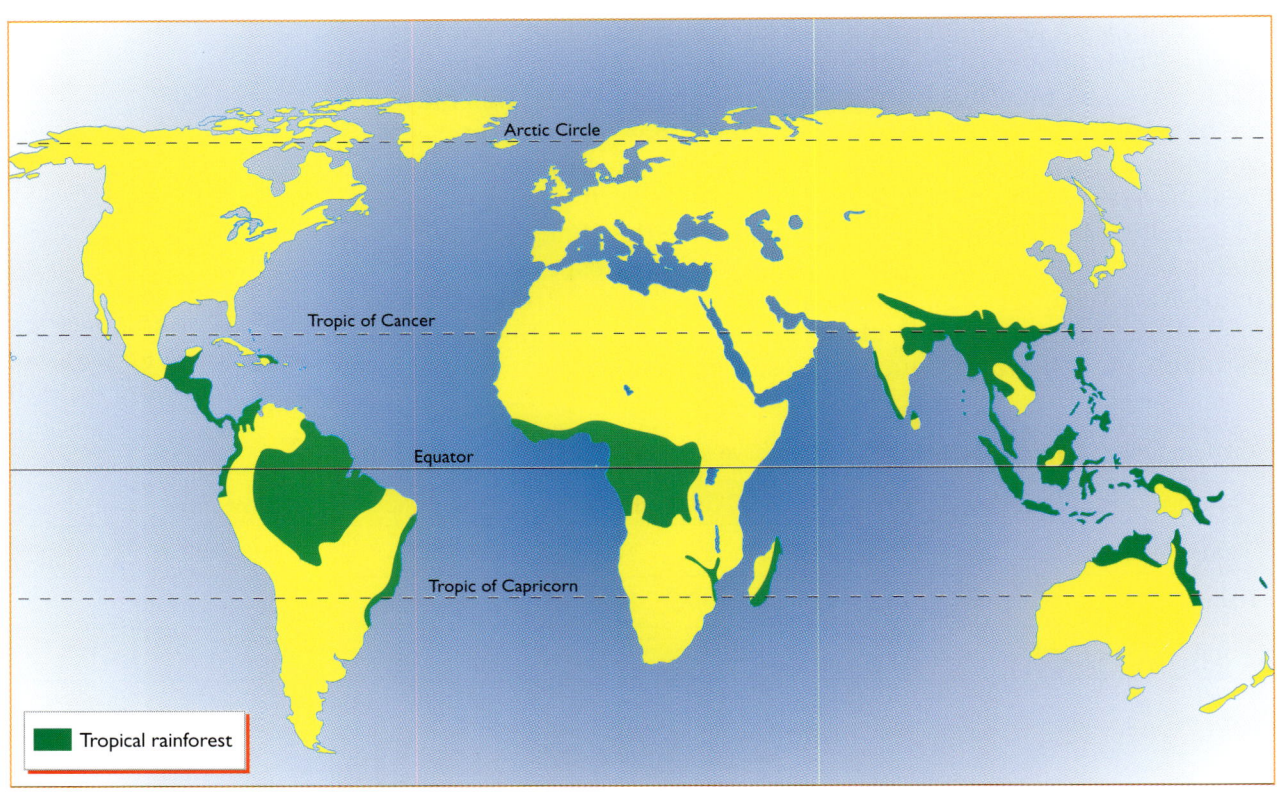

RESOURCE 3.7
World map to show distribution of tropical rain forests

RESOURCE 3.8
Aerial photo of 'Igapo' flooded forest, Amazonas State, Brazil

Deforestation

It is thought that tropical rainforests once covered as much as 20% of the Earth's land surface. Today, however, they cover only 7%, as the forests are being destroyed by people. This clearance, or deforestation, is partly the result of logging for valuable tropical hardwoods such as mahogany, teak and ebony. However, huge areas have also been cleared to make way for growing crops, cattle ranching, mining and settlement.

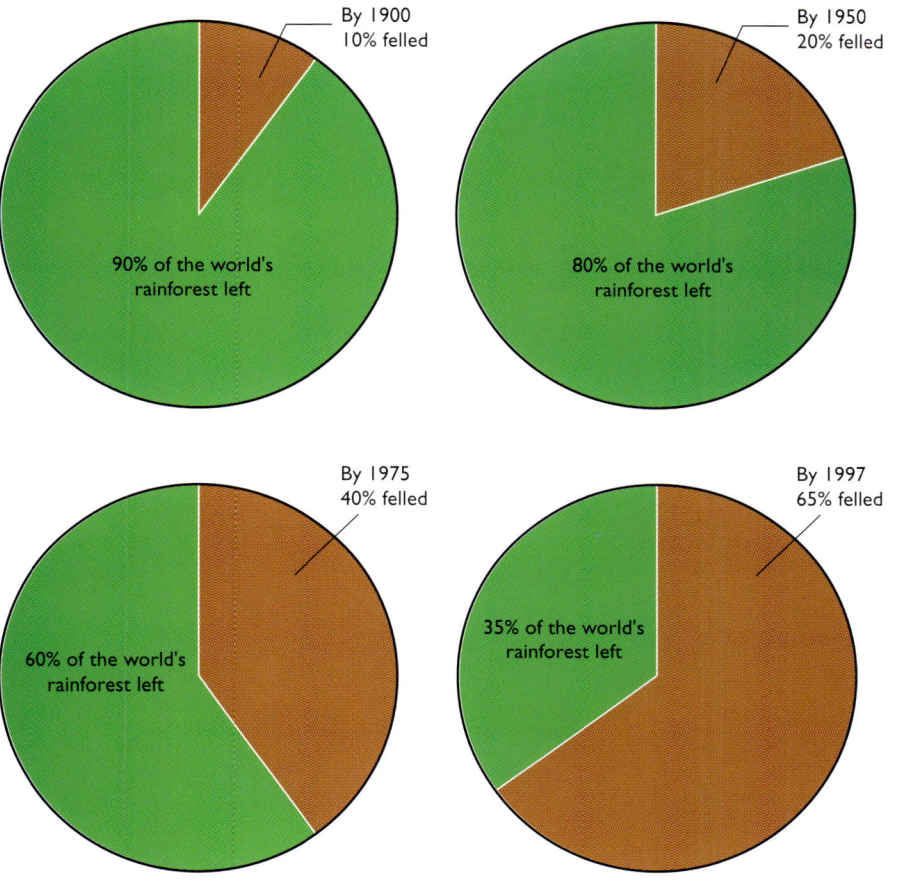

RESOURCE 3.9
Diagram to show loss of Tropical Rainforest

10. The pie charts in Resource 3.9 shows the rapid loss of the World's Rainforests, especially in the last 22 years. If the pace of deforestation continues, how much rainforest would be left by the year 2010?

The tropical rainforest in south-east Asia

It is only in the last 40 years that logging has become the main reason for the loss of tropical rainforest in countries such as Malaysia and Indonesia. Early settlers thought the area would be ideal for growing crops. However, heavy rains tore gullies into the bare soil and washed away the nutrients it contained, while the hot sun baked the bare surface to a hard, brick-like crust. The rainforests of south-east Asia have also been cleared to allow urban development, e.g. Singapore, Kuala Lumpur and Jakarta, and for rubber plantations, especially in Malaysia.

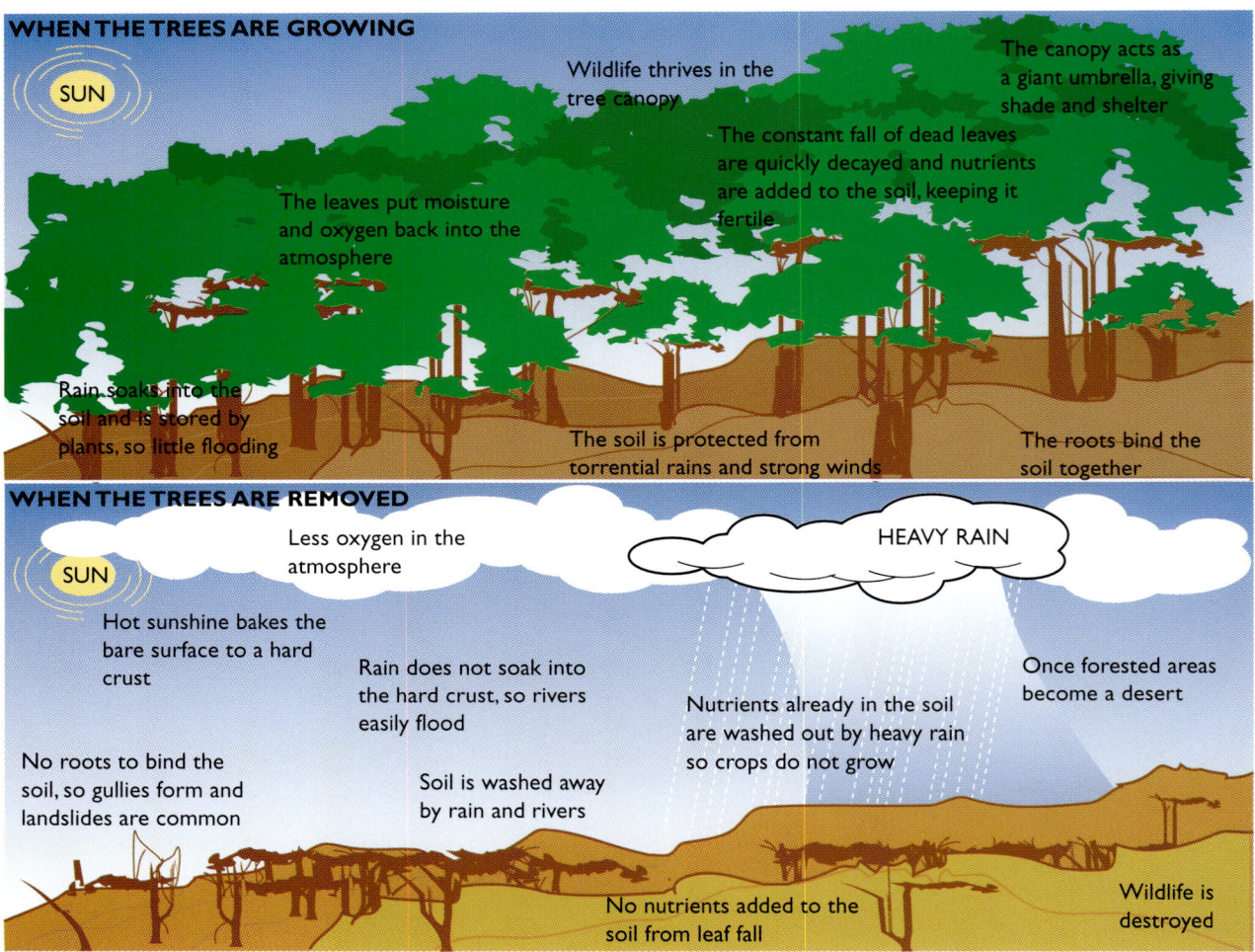

RESOURCE 3.10A AND B
'Before' and 'after' deforestation

Look at Resource 3.10A and B, which show the situation before and after deforestation.

11. Why does deforestation lead to soil erosion?

12. Do you think that rainforests need protection? Give reasons for your answer.

Tropical savannahs

With increasing distance from the sea the rainforests of the Congo basin in Africa, the Amazonian basin of South America, and northern Australia become thinner. Gradually the forests peter out into tropical grasslands. Here, rainfall is less and there are marked wet and dry seasons. The tropical grassland ecosystem consists of scattered trees, thorn scrub and tall grasses with huge herds of grazing animals and their predators.

The rainy season arrives in the 'high-sun season' – when the sun moves overhead at midday. This coincides with the summers of each hemisphere. However, the further away from the Equator the place is, the less its rainfall, and the less reliable it is. Amounts may vary sharply from year to year and sometimes it fails altogether.

RESOURCE 3.11
Tropical savannah with grazing antelope

RESOURCE 3.12
Climate Figures for Harare, Zimbabwe (approx. 16° S)

Climate Figures for Harare, Zimbabwe (approx. 16° S)												
Month	Jan	Feb	Mar	Apr	May	Jun	Jul	Aug	Sep	Oct	Nov	Dec
Temperature ° C	20.5	20.0	19.4	18.3	15.5	13.9	13.3	16.1	18.3	20.5	21.1	20.5
Rainfall mm	191	203	127	20	5	0	0	0	13	31	99	152
Total = 841 mm												
NB: As Harare is in the Southern Hemisphere the high-sun season is from October to March bringing the rainy season.												

In these areas night and daytime temperatures can be very different. In the dry season, day temperatures in the shade may be as high as 38° C, but at night they drop sharply often to less than 5° C. This is because there is no cloud cover. In the heat of the day the plants wither and dry out, rivers run dry and soils bake to a hard crust. Life only wakes up again when the rains arrive – the rivers fill with water and the plants burst into new growth.

The savannah ecosystem

The tropical grasslands in Africa are called 'savannahs'. They support vast herds of grazing animals – African elephant, zebras, wildebeest, giraffe, antelope and many more. In the dry season they must migrate over hundreds of kilometres in search of greener pastures. The herds are tracked by predators and scavengers, including lions, hyenas and jackals. Bush fires are a common hazard. They may be natural fires started by lightning, or caused deliberately in the dry season by nomadic herdsmen. This is to clear the dry vegetation so that their cattle can more easily graze the new growth when the rains arrive. The ash from the fires also acts as a fertiliser.

Many of the plants have developed ways to avoid being destroyed by grazing animals, the annual drought and frequent fires. For example, the extraordinary baobab tree (sometimes called the 'upside-down tree') has a thick bark of cork, a swollen trunk which stores water, and short branches with few leaves to reduce water loss by evaporation. Acacia trees grow here too, but are seldom grazed because of their very sharp thorns.

Throughout the savannah grasslands termite heaps are a common sight. Termites carry out a vital role as one of the many decomposers collecting, eating and digesting organic material, and returning the nutrients to the soil. Some termite heaps are several metres high and their mud walls are amazing examples of 'insect architecture', with ventilator shafts and other systems for controlling the temperature and moisture levels of their fortress.

RESOURCE 3.13
Lion with kill

13. The organisms listed below are all found in a savannah ecosystem. Rearrange the following list in the correct order for a food chain, starting with a green plant: antelope (herbivore); vulture (scavenger); termite (decomposer); lion (carnivore); savannah grass.

14. What do you think would happen to the tropical grassland ecosystem if carnivores such as lions became extinct?

15. Why are termites so important in savannah areas?

16. Is fire a problem to the savannahs?

RESOURCE 3.14
Termite heaps

Desertification

The savannah grasslands are heavily grazed by both wild and domestic animals. In such countries as Kenya, huge national game parks have been set up to save the wildlife on which the tourist industry depends.

RESOURCE 3.15
Dunes advancing on the pine wood, Coto Donana National Park, Spain

These overgrazed areas are close to the margins of hot deserts such as the Sahara and the Kalahari. These deserts are able to spread and take over the areas that once supported small amounts of farming and limited grazing. This is called 'desertification'. There is evidence that the removal of trees and other plants means that even less rain falls in these areas where the amounts were always unreliable. This has brought problems to many areas of the Sahel, a drought-prone strip that forms the southern edge of the Sahara, and more recently in southern Africa. The drought has caused famine and starvation, problems that have been made even worse by local wars in Ethiopia, Somalia and the Sudan.

International aid agencies such as Oxfam are helping to reduce the problem. They are working with local people in some of these drought-prone countries such as Burkino Faso. As well as bore holes and wind pumps to extract water to irrigate crops, dry farming methods have been developed. One very simple but effective way is to place lines of stones, a few centimetres high, across a slope. These act as mini dams trapping the water and the silt when it does rain, allowing the valuable water to soak in and help fill the water table below. The people have nicknamed them 'magic stones'.

RESOURCE 3.16
Sand dune desert, with group of Bedouin Arabs with camels

17. Read page 43. If you were a TV reporter what would you ask your film crew to take pictures of to show the causes of desertification?

18. Which do you think is best:

    a) to give foreign aid to people suffering from starvation by providing them with food, or

    b) to help people develop their own dry farming schemes? Please give your reasons.

ECOSYSTEMS

Deserts

Deserts are places where rain rarely falls. They receive less than 250 mm in a year. Like tropical rainforest, most people have a false image of deserts from films they have seen. Yes, some deserts are very sandy and incredibly hot – but there are cold deserts too. Even if the day is hot, temperatures may fall below freezing point at night. Neither are all deserts covered with sand dunes. Many are vast areas of bare rock, sand-blasted into amazing shapes by the wind. Others are huge, flat stony plains with a sparse scattering of plants such as cacti.

RESOURCE 3.17
A camel, sometimes called the ship of the desert

RESOURCE 3.18
Arizona desert in USA

19. Make a list of the difficulties that you think you would have to face if you lived in an area with a desert climate.

What all deserts have in common is that plants find it difficult to grow there. Those that do are often concentrated in oases – places where water is found that has travelled in wadis (valleys that have been cut by water but are usually dry) or where water has seeped through rocks extending from wetter mountainous areas that may be hundreds of kilometres away. Many desert plants only grow for a few days immediately after a rare rain storm. Seeds can lie asleep (dormant) in the desert for hundreds of years, awaiting a chance to grow and burst into flower if ever moisture comes their way. Cactus plants store water in their swollen stems and have extremely long roots reaching deep into the ground. Their leaves are reduced to spikes so little water can evaporate and they stop animals eating them! The sap of the huge saguaro cactus of Arizona contains a powerful poison.

Desert animals

Some animals have become adapted to live in deserts, although they may need to spend much of their lives searching for water. Many only come out in the cool of the night, sipping the dew that forms on rocks and plants. Kangaroo rats, gerbils and meerkats get much of their moisture by gnawing seeds and plant roots. The camel has been called 'the ship of the desert', a reference to the range of adaptations that these animals have to suit them for desert conditions. A camel may go for many days without water but when it does get a chance, it can drink 120 litres in about 10 minutes!

Deserts and people

Deserts are difficult places for people to live and so most deserts are empty. The Rub al Khali in Saudi Arabia, for example, means the 'Empty Quarter'. However, there are some exceptions. In Egypt, the valley of the River Nile has more people to the square kilometre than almost anywhere else on Earth! As it flows from its sources in Ethiopia and eastern Africa on its northward journey to the Mediterranean Sea, the Nile cuts across the Sahara Desert. Green crops can be grown here because the waters of the Nile are used for irrigation. The soil is rich, supplied with nutrients that were spread by the floods that used to occur here every year.

RESOURCE 3.19
Satellite picture of the Nile Valley. Plants and crops show up in red, the desert is white

Ecosystems

Today, however, the Nile is controlled by the Aswan Dam which stores the water in a huge reservoir, and floods no longer occur.

Apart from the Nile valley, some isolated settlements are seen scattered through the world's deserts. Some are villages and small towns found at oases, where water supplies are available. Others are based around oil wells, and these give rise to other settlements such as those bordering the Persian Gulf in the Middle East. Here, storage tanks and tanker loading quays, linked by pipeline to the oil wells, line the Gulf coast and have given rise to cities such as Kuwait, Bahrain and Abu Dhabi.

Traditionally the Bedouin Arabs have lived in the deserts of North Africa and the Middle East as nomads, roaming from place to place with their herds of camels, sheep and goats in search of grazing and water, or as travelling traders. Their loose flowing robes are cool and effective protection for the skin against the harmful rays of the sun.

RESOURCE 3.20
Traditional Bedouin settlers

20. Describe the ways in which people have adapted to live in desert areas.

4 THE CHANGING CLIMATE AND ENVIRONMENTAL ISSUES

> ### Key Idea
> There have been many recent changes to the Earth's climate and some are due to the activities of people and industry. Not all of the changes have been in the best interests of the planet. This chapter will examine the ways the climate has been affected, and some of the measures taken to reverse the damage.

Constant change

There is strong evidence to suggest that ever since the Earth was first formed 4,600 million years ago, the conditions in the atmosphere that cause climate have frequently changed.

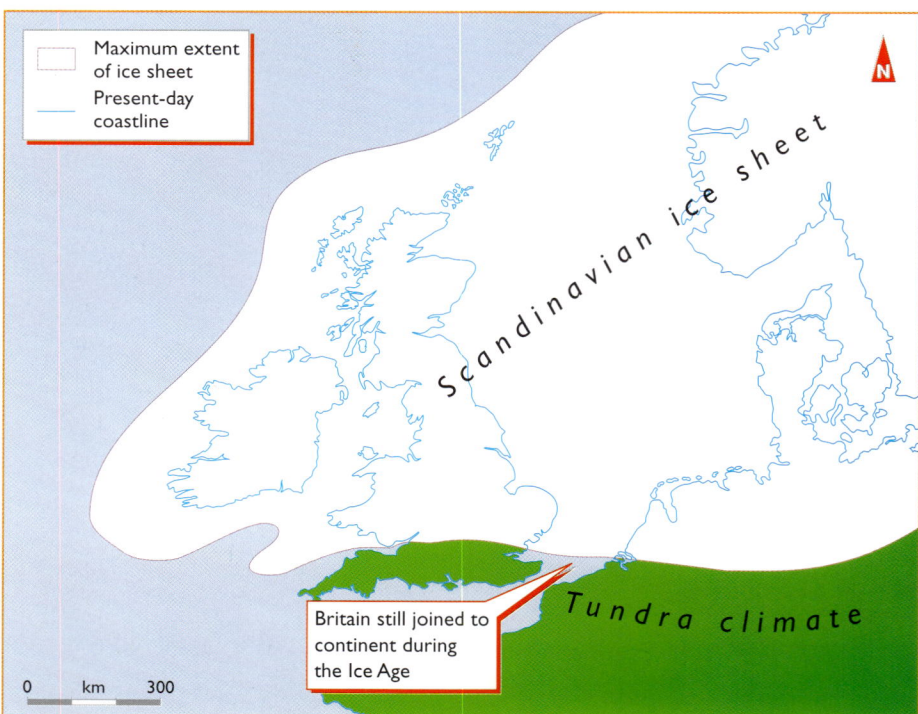

RESOURCE 4.1 Where ice sheets were in British Isles at time of maximum extent

The Changing Climate and Environmental Issues

18,000 years ago – a very short time when compared with the age of the Earth – ice sheets up to 3 km thick covered much of Britain and the rest of Europe, Asia and North America. In the Southern Hemisphere too, large areas were ice covered.

For some reason, which scientists have not yet fully explained, the atmosphere began to warm up around 18,000 years ago. Most of the ice sheets melted and sea levels began to rise dramatically. Only 7,000 years ago the rising sea levels cut Britain off from France when the sea broke through the chalk ridge that linked the white cliffs of Dover to Cap Blanc Nez near Calais, creating the Straits of Dover.

More recently temperatures and amounts of rainfall have also varied. In the 10th and 11th Centuries AD, at the time of the Viking invasions of Britain, temperatures in Europe were similar to, or even a little warmer than today. But by the middle of the 15th Century the climate had become very much colder. From about 1450 to 1850, Britain and other parts of Europe experienced a time that has been called 'The Little Ice Age' with much hard frost, causing rivers to freeze over. The winters of 1795 and 1814, were especially cold, and 'Frost Fairs' were held on the frozen River Thames in London. It is also known that glaciers in the high mountains of the Alps and Pyrenees were able to advance during this time.

RESOURCE 4.2
Volcanic eruptions such as Mt. Vesuvius (pictured left) throw huge amounts of ash into the atmosphere and may cause the climate to be colder for shorter periods

1. Try to locate whereabouts you live on the map shown in Resource 4.1. Would the area have been ice covered during the Ice Age?

2. From an encyclopaedia or a book on physical geography find out what kind of features glaciers and ice sheets created in the landscape.

Why does the climate change?

There are many explanations for these changes to our climate, but no one is really sure why it happens. Perhaps the Earth is wobbling on its axis or its orbit around the Sun varies, so that for part of the year it is further away than normal. Solar activity by Sun spots may also provide part of the answer.

Volcanic eruptions throwing massive amounts of gases and volcanic ash high into the atmosphere can also cause climate change. From diaries kept during the 18th Century we know that the Laki volcano near Iceland erupted in 1783. During that summer the sunsets were remarkable for their vivid colours, and even at midday over Britain the sun appeared rusty red as it shone through the high clouds of volcanic ash. The winter of 1783/84 that followed was even colder than usual, with hard frosts and snow from Christmas to May, even in southern England. More recently very colourful sunsets have been experienced due to the eruption of Mt. St Helens, USA.

RESOURCE 4.3
South African sunset

Climate change and people

It seems increasingly likely, however, that some recent changes to the Earth's climate are due to the activities of people. On page 18 'smog' (smoke fog) is described, caused by air pollution by fumes from burning coal, industry and car exhausts.

3. Carry out a survey among your class or tutor group. Ask them:

    a) How many journeys do you make from your home each week?

    b) How are these journeys made – by car? – by coach or bus? by train? by cycle? on foot?

4. Keeping your personal safety in mind how many of the car journey's you make each week could be made instead by public transport, cycle or on foot?

Air pollution

Every time we switch on an electric light, burn coal, and use petrol or diesel in a car, we are using up 'energy'. Most of this energy comes from 'fossil fuels' – coal, oil and natural gas. These fuels have been stored in the Earth's rocks. They were formed from the fossilised remains of plants and animals that lived millions of years ago. As this fossil fuel is used up to make electricity, to heat our homes or propel our vehicles, polluting gases are also released.

Smoke, car exhaust fumes and gases from power stations contain chemicals such as sulphur dioxide, oxides of nitrogen, carbon monoxide and carbon dioxide. These escape into the atmosphere as pollutants. Polluted air is a health hazard, causing many problems including asthma, bronchitis, and, in extreme cases, heart attacks. It also causes acid rain. Most of the time we are not very aware of air pollution. We may smell it, but most of the polluting gases are invisible. However, there are tell-tale signs we can look for. Lichens, the grey-green or orange coloured crusts or hairy tassels that grow on rocks, stones and trees are very sensitive to air pollution. The more lichens there are growing in an area, the better the quality of its air.

RESOURCE 4.4
Smoking chimneys causing air pollution

Acid rain

RESOURCE 4.5
Eroded limestone statue

RESOURCE 4.6
Trees killed by acid rain

Rain water is a natural, but very weak acid, as dissolved carbon dioxide gas from the air forms a very dilute solution of carbonic acid. However, sulphur dioxide and oxides of nitrogen in polluted air join with the naturally produced gases in the atmosphere from volcanoes, decaying vegetation and cattle. These gases also dissolve in the moisture in the atmosphere, forming stronger acids such as sulphuric and nitric acids which fall as 'acid rain'.

5. What are the causes of acid rain?

6. List some of the main problems caused by acid rain. Are there any clues that show that acid rain falls in the area where you live?

The Changing Climate and Environmental Issues

The example of Sweden's lakes shows that acid rain can kill fish in rivers and lakes. It also kills trees, insects and other wildlife. Large areas of the Czech Republic, once forested, are now bare of trees, and in Germany's Black Forest many trees are sick or dying. They are killed by acid rain caused by fumes from industry. It also damages statues and buildings by dissolving away stonework.

This is an international problem, as the source of the pollution causing the acidity may be many kilometres from the country affected. For example, it is known that the acid rain that falls on Sweden comes from air pollution in the British Isles.

RESOURCE 4.7
Sweetening an acid lake with Agricultural Lime

Sweden has some 40,000 lakes. 4,000 of these now have no fish-life because they are too acidic. Another 18,000 are partly acidic.

7. Draw a pie graph to show these figures. Using compasses, draw a circle with a radius of 5 cm. Draw a line from the edge of the circle to the centre point. Use a protractor to mark off angles of 36° and 198° from this first line at the centre point. Draw lines at these angles from the centre point to the edge of the circle. Colour in the 2 wedges, that of 36° in a dark colour and the second wedge (198° − 36° = 162°) in a paler colour. Leave the remaining wedge (also 162°) uncoloured. Add a key:

Dark-coloured wedge: 10% of Sweden's lakes have no fish life, water is too acidic;
Pale-coloured wedge: 45% of Sweden's lakes are partly acidic;
Uncoloured wedge: Only 45% of Sweden's lakes remain 'normal'.

Global warming and the greenhouse effect

Global warming is caused by what has been called **'the greenhouse effect'**. As the Sun shines, short-wave heat energy is radiated through space. These short-wave rays pass through glass into a greenhouse, but the glass will not allow the long-wave rays radiated back to pass through, and they make the greenhouse warm as they are trapped inside. In the same way the Sun's rays pass through the Earth's atmosphere until they reach the surface. Here, the rays heat up the rocks, soil and water until the Earth's surface starts to radiate heat back again into the atmosphere. The heat radiated by the Earth's surface is in the form of long-waves and would radiate back into space. However, they are trapped in the atmosphere by carbon dioxide and other 'greenhouse gases', which act just like the greenhouse glass. Carbon dioxide is just one of several 'greenhouse gases'. Methane is another, and is produced by the natural decay of plants (it is called 'marsh gas'), and as a waste product from animals digesting their food.

Since 1860 there has been a temperature rise across the entire planet of about 0.5° C. In the same time, the amount of carbon dioxide in the atmosphere air has gone up by 72.5%. As this continues to increase, it is predicted that global temperatures will rise by another 1° C between the year 2000 and 2030, and by 3° C by the year 2100!

RESOURCE 4.8
How the Greenhouse Effect works

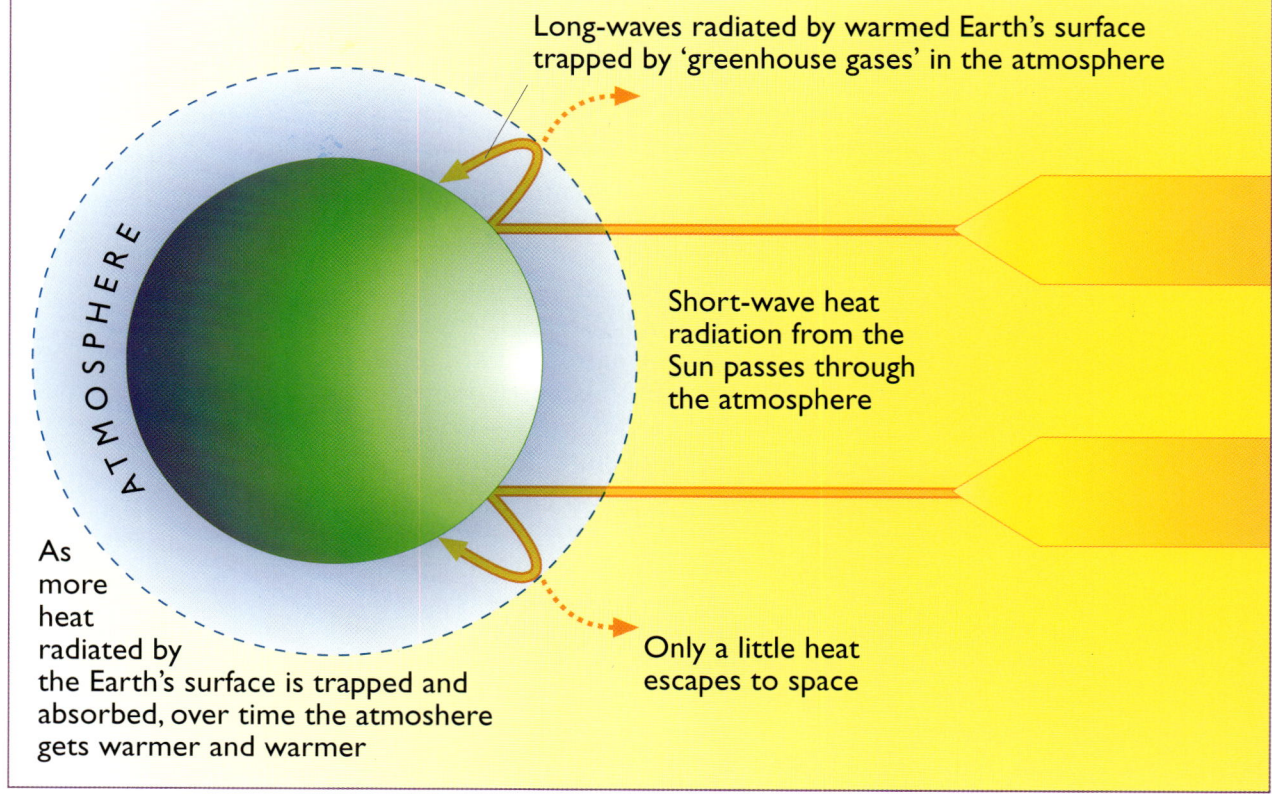

The Changing Climate and Environmental Issues

Although global warming is still not 'proved', most scientists now agree that the Earth's atmosphere is getting warmer. This is almost certainly being caused by rising levels of carbon dioxide and the other greenhouse gases released into the air by such human activities as burning fossil fuels.

If the predicted global warming does take place, the world's vegetation zones will also change and sea levels will rise. This rise would partly be due to the amount of water added to the oceans by melting glaciers and ice sheets, but also because the water in the oceans will expand as it is warmed up.

Holes in the ozone layer

Until recently *chloro-fluoro-carbons* or 'CFCs' were used to provide the 'squirt' in aerosol sprays, as a coolant in air conditioning units and refrigerators, and in the manufacture of polystyrene food containers used by fast-food sellers for keeping hamburgers and similar foods warm. When CFCs are released into the atmosphere they cause yet another problem for the Earth's atmosphere – **holes in the ozone layer**.

RESOURCE 4.9
Diagram of ozone hole

Throughout the world there has been a massive rise in the use of CFCs since 1950. When CFC gases drift into the upper atmosphere the chlorine they contain is released. This reacts with ozone and destroys it. The ozone layer is a very thin and fragile layer of ozone gas in the atmosphere. It encircles the planet at a height of about 20 km and performs a very important job – it absorbs and filters out most of the harmful ultra-violet rays which are radiated by the Sun.

8. In groups draw up action plans for ways in which we might reduce the damage we all cause to the environment by wasting energy and raw materials.

9. If the sea level continues to rise at the present rate, what do you think will happen to millions of people living in low-lying areas?

If too much ultra-violet radiation were to reach the Earth's surface, the growth of plants would be severely damaged. We depend on such a great variety of crops for our food. If production of these were to be reduced, then there would be widespread starvation. Too much exposure to ultra-violet radiation can also cause skin cancer and damage to people's eyesight. Thus, without the protection of the ozone layer, it is probable that there would be no life as we know it on this planet.

In 1985 scientists from the British Antarctic Survey studying the atmosphere discovered that, in just 30 years, the amount of ozone gas in the layer over Antarctica had fallen by 50%. Later, readings from satellites confirmed these findings and also warned that the ozone layer over the Arctic was damaged too.

RESOURCE 4.10
Cricketer with sun-block smeared face

Solving the problem

There are now several international agreements banning the use of CFCs in order to prevent further damage to the ozone layer. So far, putting these agreements into action has been slow in some less developed countries. In the UK, different chemicals are now used in aerosols, refrigerators and air conditioners, and care is taken to remove CFCs from old refrigerators before recycling them. However, it will be years before the problem is fully overcome.

Seasonal weather forecasts

Much research is being carried out on how to produce 'long-range' forecasts. Meteorologists know that weather patterns are controlled by the condition of the atmosphere. This is influenced by the surface temperature of the oceans. In particular they are trying to understand the causes and effects of an event called 'El Niño'. If they can solve this mystery then long-term weather forecasting could become a reality.

10. It has been suggested that it would be of great value if meteorologists could find a way of accurately predicting weather conditions some months ahead. How would an accurate long-term weather forecast:

   a) help us when deciding where to go and what to do for our holidays?

   b) help clothing manufacturers and shopkeepers?

   c) help farmers?

The Changing Climate and Environmental Issues

Many short-term climatic changes are closely linked to a huge pool of warm water, about 200 metres deep, found in the tropical parts of the Pacific Ocean. Roughly every 5 years this warm water shifts from its normal position close to Indonesia, and drifts eastwards towards South America. It arrives at the coast of Ecuador and Peru around Christmas time, and so the local fishermen have nicknamed the event 'El Niño' which means 'The Christ Child'.

RESOURCE 4.11A
Sea level and temperature in the Pacific in January 1997 before an El Niño event

When El Niño occurs it has a strong effect on the world's weather, especially in those countries that fringe the Pacific. In normal years the warm water is located around northern Australia, Indonesia and south-east Asia. It causes low pressure and heavy rainfall across south-east Asia – the tropical monsoon. However, during an El Niño year these warm waters and their linked low pressure move to the coast of South America, and the normal Low over south-east Asia is replaced by a High.

This reverses the normal direction of the Trade Winds and triggers torrential rain in Mexico and Ecuador, causing widespread flooding and landslides, while the normally wet areas of south-east Asia suffer from disastrous droughts! During the El Niño event of 1997–98, the unusual high pressure and drought over south-east Asia trapped the smoke from many hundreds of forest fires in Indonesia and caused widespread smog from Malaysia to the Philippines. The disastrous crash of a jet plane and the collision of two ships in the area were blamed on the poor visibility.

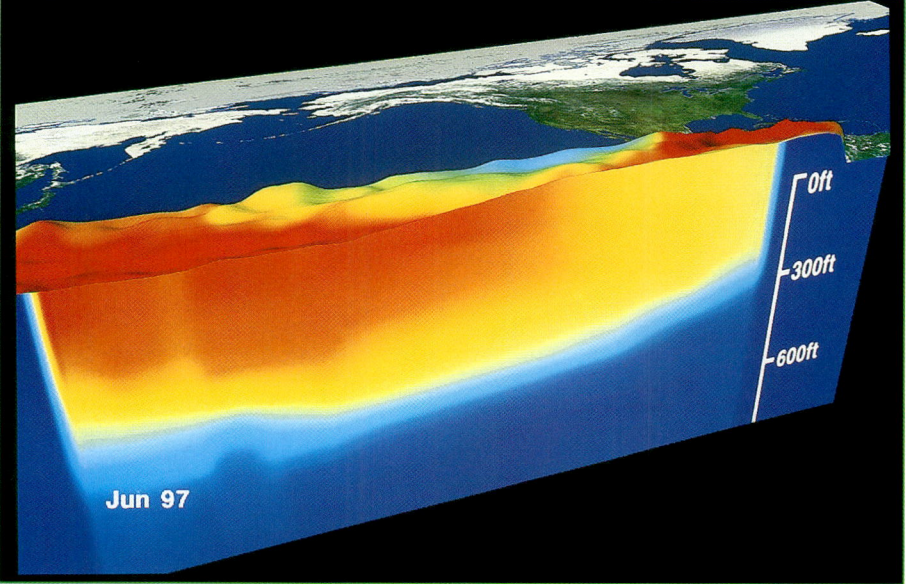

RESOURCE 4.11B
Sea level and temperature in the Pacific in June 1997 during an El Niño event

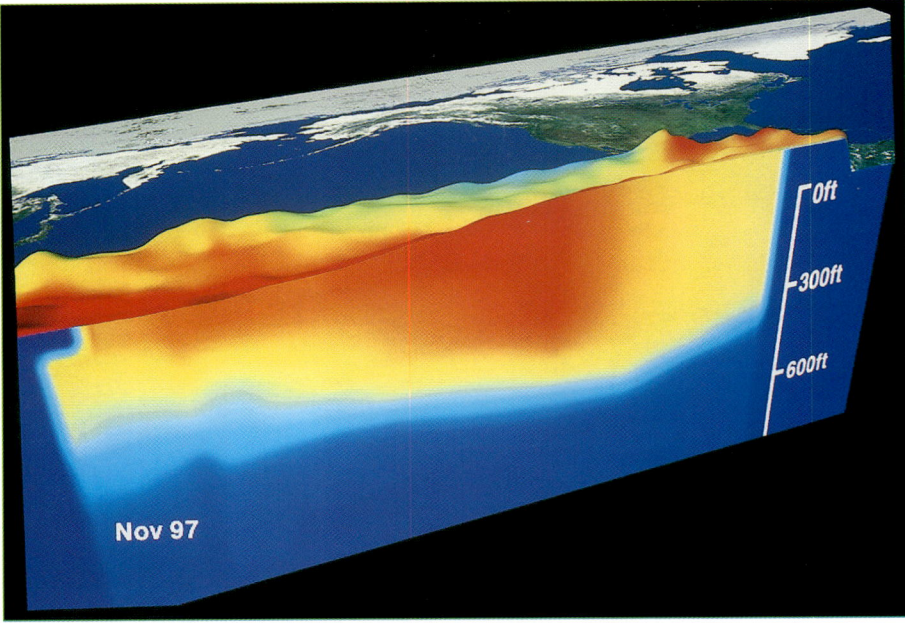

RESOURCE 4.11C
Sea level and temperature in the Pacific in November 1997 during an El Niño event

El Niño may affect the northern hemisphere too, and is the cause of stormy weather and strong surf in California, while the Sahel and the southern part of Africa experience drought conditions. El Niño may also be linked to mild winters in western Europe and the British Isles.

Although El Niño is an event with a long history, in recent years its influence on global climates appears to have been getting stronger, and its occurrence more frequent. Some conservation organisations, such as Friends of the Earth, are suggesting that this is no coincidence but is an inevitable result of global warming caused by the release of huge quantities of greenhouse gases such as carbon dioxide from burning fossil fuels.

11. What happens to the surface temperatures of the Pacific Ocean during El Niño years?
12. Why is the event called El Niño?
13. How does El Niño alter the weather conditions:
    a) in Indonesia
    b) in Peru
    c) in Britain?

RESOURCE 4.11D
Sea level and temperature in the Pacific in March 1998 during an El Niño event

GLOSSARY

acid rain Rain that falls as dilute nitric and/or sulphuric acid, because moisture in the air has dissolved nitrogen oxides and/or sulphur dioxide and other polluting gases released by car exhaust and industrial fumes.

adaptations Features that have developed in a plant or animal that equip it to live in a particular climate or ecosystem in a certain way, e.g. as a carnivore in the tropical rainforest.

air masses A large area of air that has rested in a particular part of the world long enough to take on its temperature and moisture character, e.g. warm and moist, or cold and dry.

air pressure The weight of air pressing down on a place usually measured in millibars (mbs). If air is rising, air pressure is low; if it is sinking, pressure will be high.

anticyclone An area of high air pressure – a 'high pressure' weather system.

Arctic Circle The line of latitude $66\frac{1}{2}°$ North in the Equator that borders the Arctic. The equivalent in the Southern Hemisphere is the Antarctic Circle, $66\frac{1}{2}°$ South.

atmosphere The layer of gases that surrounds the Earth. It is a mixture of oxygen (21%), nitrogen (78%), with 1% of 'other gases' including carbon dioxide, the 'inert gases' and variable amounts of water vapour.

avalanche A mass of snow, ice and rock that suddenly slides down the side of a high mountain. It may engulf skiers and mountaineers.

axis An imaginary line through the Earth from the North to the South Pole around which the planet appears to spin.

barograph An instrument that automatically records air pressure in the form of a graph.

barometer An instrument for measuring air pressure. It is usually graduated in millibars or millimetres of mercury.

Beaufort Scale A scale from 0 (dead calm) to 12 (hurricane) used for assessing wind speeds using easily seen movements of tree branches, etc. Wind speeds are also measured in kph by an anemometer.

carbon dioxide One of the gases in the air. It is used by the leaves of plants, where it is combined with hydrogen and oxygen to make sugars using the energy in sunlight.

carnivore An animal that eats meat such as a lion or sparrowhawk.

CFCs Short for 'chloro-fluoro-carbons'. These chemicals were used in aerosol sprays, as a coolant in refrigerators and air-conditioning units, and in the manufacture of polystyrene fast-food packaging. CFCs cause holes in the ozone layer in the upper atmosphere.

climate The 'average weather' of a place, based on records over at least 35 years.

cloud Clouds consist of millions of tiny ice crystals or water droplets, about 20 microns in diameter, suspended in the air.

cold front The junction between a warm and a cold air mass, in which the colder air is advancing. Shown on a weather map by a line marked with triangles. Often brings a belt of rain and thunderstorms.

condensation The process by which water droplets in a cloud, fog or dew are formed when water vapour in the air is cooled, condenses, and changes from a gas to a liquid.

conifers Mainly evergreen trees with needle-like leaves and cones such as pine and spruce.

convection The movement that takes place in air or water when it is heated. Convectional rain is the result of air rising over a warm surface, often as thunderstorms.

cumulonimbus cloud A thunder cloud. They form when a cloud extends so high in the atmosphere that its top is made of ice crystals. This gives it an 'anvil-headed' appearance.

deciduous Deciduous trees shed their leaves in autumn. It is the way in which trees such as the oak survive the cold of winter.

decomposers Bacteria, fungi and other organisms that break down dead plant and animal matter, recycling the chemicals from which it was made.

deforestation The clearance of forests. Deforestation of tropical rainforests has become a major environmental issue.

depression An area of low air pressure – a 'low pressure weather system'.

dewpoint The temperature at which water vapour condenses into liquid form.

Easterlies The Polar easterly winds that are caused by subsiding air near the Poles returning towards the Equator.

ecosystem A living system of plants and animals and their physical environment.

El Niño An irregular event in which warm water in the Pacific Ocean around south-east Asia moves towards the coast of South America. It arrives at Christmas time and 'El Niño' means 'The Christ Child'. This event disrupts the world's normal climate patterns.

evaporation The process by which water changes from liquid form to water vapour – a gas – when it is warmed.

fog A cloud of water droplets at ground level. Visibility is less than 1,000 metres.

food chain A chain of feeding that starts with green plants (the food producers), eaten (consumed) by herbivores that in turn are eaten by carnivores. Food chains transfer energy from one organism to another in an ecosystem.

fossil fuels Coal, oil and natural gas are natural resources found in the rocks. They are formed from the fossil remains of plants and animals that lived on Earth millions of years ago. When they are burnt they release huge quantities of carbon dioxide and other gases into the atmosphere.

global warming The gradual warming of the Earth's atmosphere as a result of air pollution from greenhouse gases, released by a variety of human activities.

greenhouse effect Like glass in a greenhouse, certain gases such as carbon dioxide and methane released into the atmosphere trap outgoing heat radiation from the Earth's surface and may be causing global warming.

hail Balls of ice that fall from thunder clouds in which strong updrafts (turbulence) have circulated the hailstone many times. Hailstones have several layers, as their outer surfaces freeze and thaw each time they meet with cold and warm air.

haze A very thin mist due to dispersed smoke, dust particles or widely spaced water droplets suspended in the atmosphere. Visibility is more than 2,000 metres.

hemisphere Half a sphere, and a term used to describe the two halves of the Earth either side of the Equator – the Northern Hemisphere and the Southern Hemisphere.

herbivore An animal which eats grass or other plants, e.g. rabbit, elephant, deer, sheep, cow.

high pressure A weather system, also called an anticyclone or a 'High', in which air is sinking towards the surface. It usually has calm, fine weather, but in winter can bring frost and fog.

hot spot A small area of the Earth's surface that has become heated more than the area around it by the Sun's rays. Bare rock and fields, concrete and tarmac often heat more quickly than areas of crops, woodland and water. Hot spots cause bubbles of air to rise that may cause thunderstorms.

humidity levels The amount of water vapour in the air. Warm air can hold more water vapour than cold air. Air with a 100% humidity level is said to be saturated.

hurricane A violent tropical or sub-tropical storm caused by very low pressure, with torrential rain and winds of more than 118 kph. Hurricanes have a calm 'eye' at their centre. Also called 'typhoons' and 'cyclones'.

hydrocarbons Petrol, diesel and other products made from crude oil are hydrocarbons. Strong sunlight causes a chemical reaction in unburned hydrocarbons in car exhaust fumes, causing smog in cities, e.g. Athens, Los Angeles.

ice Frozen water. Water changes its form from a liquid to solid ice when it freezes at 0° C. When ice is warmed it melts, and changes back to liquid water.

isobars A line on a weather map joining places with the same air pressure. Isobars are usually drawn at intervals of 4 millibars (mbs).

isotherm A line on a climate map joining places with the same temperature.

jet streams Very fast moving air currents high in the atmosphere.

lightning A massive electric spark in a cloud or from a cloud to the ground. It is caused by the build-up of opposite electrical charges. The rapid heating of the air around the lightning flash to over 20,000° C makes it expand rapidly, causing a clap of thunder.

low pressure A weather system, also called a depression or a 'Low'. Air is rising in the atmosphere and cooling. Low pressure usually brings cloudy weather, probably with rain or snow. Hurricanes and tornadoes are the result of extreme low pressure.

maximum (max.)/minimum (min.) temperature The highest and lowest temperature recorded in 24 hours, a week, month or year. A max./min. thermometer has metal indicators to show these temperatures.

mean temperature The 'average' temperature. The 'mean temperature for 24 hours' is calculated by adding the max. and min. and dividing by 2. For the 'mean monthly temperature', add together the month's mean daily temperatures and divide by the number of days.

Meteorological Office The UK's national weather service at Bracknell, Berkshire.

methane A gas produced by rotting animal and plant remains and by the digestion of food by animals. It is one of the 'Greenhouse gases'.

millibars (mbs) A unit, measured by a barometer, of the weight of air over a particular point of the Earth's surface. On average, air pressure at sea level is 1 kilogram per square centimetre = 1,000 mbs.

mist Caused by tiny water droplets suspended in the air. It is thinner than a fog and visibility is between 1,000 and 2,000 metres.

occluded front If a cold front has 'overtaken' a warm front, the warmer air is forced to rise. An occluded front is represented on a weather chart by a line marked with both the triangle and semicircle symbols. Occluded fronts may bring a belt of heavy rain.

oktas Eighths of the area of sky, used for estimating the amount of cloud cover. If the sky is half cloud covered then it is said to be $\frac{4}{8}$ oktas.

oxygen 21% of the air we breathe is oxygen. It is vital for the support of life and is released by green leaves when making food from carbon dioxide and water using the energy of sunlight.

ozone A gas in the atmosphere that forms a thin, natural layer, between 15 and 40 km above the Earth's surface. It absorbs most of the harmful ultraviolet rays from the Sun. Holes in the ozone layer are now appearing each year above the polar regions due to ozone gas being destroyed by CFCs released into the atmosphere.

precipitation A general name given to drizzle, rain, snow and hail falling on the Earth's surface. On average, a raindrop is 2,000 microns (2 mm) in diameter.

predators Animals such as lions and falcons that hunt and eat other animals.

pollution Damage caused by substances released into the environment by human activities. These often come from industrial processes, particularly when fossil fuels are burnt.

'relief' or 'mountain' rain Rainfall caused by air being forced to rise and cool over an area of high relief – hills or mountains. The area beyond the hills where the air descends receives less precipitation and is called a 'rain-shadow area'.

scavengers Animals like hyenas and buzzards that search for and eat dead animals.

sleet Partially melted snow, where the precipitation falls as a mixture of raindrops and snowflakes.

smog A 'smoke fog' caused either by large amounts of smoke mixed with fog, or by a chemical reaction caused by sunlight in the unburned hydrocarbons from car exhaust fumes.

snow Small, hexagonal crystals of ice. No two snow flakes are the same! Usually many crystals link together to form larger, feather-like snowflakes that are heavy enough to fall as precipitation.

tornado A narrow, violently-spinning, column of air rising from the ground to a storm cloud, that can have wind speeds exceeding 450 kph! Also called 'twisters'.

Trade Winds Part of the global wind system. The Trade Winds that blow in sub-tropical areas from the high pressure zone around latitudes 30° towards the low pressure around the Equator. However, they are deflected from a north–south alignment by the rotation of the Earth and blow from the north-east in the Northern Hemisphere and south-east in the Southern Hemisphere.

tropic The lines of latitude $23\frac{1}{2}°$ North of the Equator (the Tropic of Cancer) and $23\frac{1}{2}°$ South of the Equator (the Tropic of Capricorn). Areas between these two tropics are referred to as 'tropical'.

warm front The junction between a warm and a cold air mass, and represents the line along which the warmer air is advancing. Shown on a weather map by a line marked with semi-circles. Often brings a belt of rain.

Water vapour Water in the atmosphere in the form of an invisible gas. The amount of water vapour in the air is referred to as its humidity level.

Weather The temperature, windspeeds, cloud cover, sunshine or precipitation experienced by a place at a particular moment. Weather is caused by the condition of the atmosphere.

Westerlies Part of the global wind system. They blow in mid-latitudes from the high pressure around 30° latitude towards the Poles, but are deflected by the rotation of the Earth. Thus, they blow from the south-west North of the Equator, and from the north-west south of the Equator.

windchill Strong winds make the air temperature feel colder than it really is. This is called the 'windchill factor'.